An invitation to the reader

Across the millennia, there have been periods of sudden acceleration in the otherwise gradual progress of civilization— times of explosive growth marked by intense cultural, social, and technological change. From the far reaches of early recorded history to recent centuries, the emergence of the world's great religions has driven leaps in human progress. These outpourings of creativity have resulted in some of humanity's most impressive and enduring achievements in the arts, architecture, governance, law, literature, and science.

Members of the Bahá'í Faith, representing virtually every country and territory on the planet, see humanity as standing on the cusp of just such a great societal shift—one that will be global in scope. The next and necessary stage in humanity's continuing ascent is the unification of all nations and peoples in a peaceful and just global civilization—one that welcomes and honors all, benefiting from the unique cultural and religious heritage each brings to the whole.

Humanity has passed through the stages of its infancy and childhood and now stands at the threshold of its collective maturity. The conflict, turbulence, and confusion we are experiencing today are features of a transitional period that can be likened to adolescence. Old and outmoded attitudes and habits of thinking are being swept away and new patterns of thought and action are gradually taking root.

Bahá'u'lláh (1817-1892), the Founder of the Bahá'í Faith, advanced the claim that His mission was to educate humanity for this long-awaited stage of global civilization. This coming age, He claimed, is nothing less than the era of worldwide peace and justice foretold in sacred scriptures since ancient times.

Bahá'u'lláh revealed a profound spiritual vision, revolutionary principles, and practical approaches to lead humanity through its treacherous adolescence into maturity. Centered on the fundamental principle of the oneness of humanity, His teachings offer us hopeful new ways to view our place and purpose in the world. Bahá'u'lláh's life and writings have given rise to a worldwide Bahá'í community committed to learning how to put His teachings into practice.

In the following pages, we invite you to explore the history, beliefs, and practices of the Bahá'í Faith.

CONTENTS

34

What Bahá'ís believe

46

Belief in action

72

The Covenant and the Administrative Order of the Bahá'í Faith

88

Universal peace

Religion *in an* EVER-ADVANCING civilization

"The purpose of religion ... is to establish unity and concord amongst the peoples of the world; make it not the cause of dissension and strife."

— BAHÁ'U'LLÁH

The world's great faiths have animated civilizations throughout history. Each affirms the existence of an all-loving God and opens the doors of understanding to the spiritual dimension of life. Each cultivates the love of God and of humanity in the human heart and seeks to bring out the noblest qualities and aspirations of the human being. Each has beckoned humankind to higher forms of civilization.

Over the thousands of years of humanity's collective infancy and adolescence, the systems of shared belief brought by the world's great religions have enabled people to unite and create bonds of trust and cooperation at ever-higher levels of social organization—from the family, to the tribe, to the city-state and nation. As the human race moves toward a global civilization, this power of religion to promote cooperation and propel cultural evolution can perhaps be better understood today than ever before. It is an insight that is increasingly being recognized and is affirmed in the work of evolutionary psychologists and cultural anthropologists.

The teachings of the Founders of the world's religions have inspired breathtaking achievements in literature, architecture, art, and music. They have fostered the promo-tion of reason, science, and education. Their moral principles have been translated into universal codes of law, regulating and elevating human relationships. These uniquely endowed individuals are referred to as "Manifestations of God" in the Bahá'í writings, and include (among others) Krishna, Moses, Zoroaster, Buddha, Jesus Christ, Muhammad, the Báb, and Bahá'u'lláh. History provides countless examples of how these Figures have awakened in whole populations capacities to love, to forgive, to create, to dare greatly, to overcome prejudice, to sacrifice for the common good, and to discipline the impulses of humanity's baser instincts. These achievements can be recognized as the common spiritual heritage of the human race.

Today, humanity faces the limits of a social order inadequate to meet the compelling challenges of a world that has virtually shrunk to the level of a neighborhood. On this small planet, sovereign nations find themselves caught between cooperation and competition. The well-being of humanity and of the environment are too often compromised for national self-interest. Propelled by competing ideologies, divided by various constructs of "us" versus "them," the people of the world are plunged into

one crisis after another—brought on by war, terrorism, prejudice, oppression, economic disparity, and environmental upheaval, among other causes.

Bahá'u'lláh—as the latest in the series of divinely inspired moral educators Who have guided humanity from age to age—has proclaimed that humanity is now approaching its long-awaited stage of maturity: unity at the global level of social organization. He provides a vision of the oneness of humanity, a moral framework, and teachings that, founded on the harmony of science and religion, directly address today's problems. He points the way to the next stage of human social evolution. He offers to the peoples of the world a unifying story consistent with our scientific understanding of reality. He calls on us to recognize our common humanity, to see ourselves as members of one family, to end estrangement and prejudice, and to come together. By doing so, all peoples and every social group can be protagonists in shaping their own future and, ultimately, a just and peaceful global civilization.

One humanity, one unfolding faith

We live in a time of rapid, often unsettling change. People today survey the transformations underway in the world with mixed feelings of anticipation and dread, of hope and anxiety. In the societal, economic, and political realms, essential questions about our identity and the nature of the relationships that bind us together are being raised to a degree not seen in decades.

"All men have been created to carry forward an ever-advancing civilization."

—BAHÁ'U'LLÁH

At the heart of
Bahá'u'lláh's
message are
two core ideas:

first

the incontrovertible
truth that humanity
is one

second

humanity's great
faiths have come
from one common
Source and are
expressions of one
unfolding religion

Progress in science and technology represents hope for addressing many of the challenges that are emerging, but such progress is itself a powerful force of disruption, changing the ways we make choices, learn, organize, work, and play, and raising moral questions that have not been encountered before. Some of the most formidable problems facing humanity—those dealing with the human condition and requiring moral and ethical decisions—cannot be solved through science and technology alone, however critical their contributions.

The teachings of Bahá'u'lláh help us understand the transformations underway. At the heart of His message are two core ideas. First is the incontrovertible truth that humanity is one, a truth that embodies the very spirit of the age, for without it, it is impossible to build a truly just and peaceful world. Second is the understanding that humanity's great faiths have come from one common Source and are expressions of one unfolding religion.

In His writings, Bahá'u'lláh raised a call to the leaders of nations, to religious figures, and to the generality of humankind to give due importance to the place of religion in human advancement. All of the Founders of the world's great religions, He explained, proclaim the same faith. He described religion as "the chief instrument for the establishment of order in the world and of tranquility amongst its peoples" and referred to it as a "radiant light and an impregnable stronghold for the protection and welfare of the peoples of the world." In another of His Tablets, He states that "the purpose of religion is to safeguard the interests and promote the unity of the human race, and to foster the spirit of love and fellowship amongst men." "The religion of God and His divine law," He further explains, "are the most potent instruments and the surest of

all means for the dawning of the light of unity amongst men. The progress of the world, the development of nations, the tranquility of peoples, and the peace of all who dwell on earth are among the principles and ordinances of God. Religion bestoweth upon man the most precious of all gifts, offereth the cup of prosperity, imparteth eternal life, and showereth imperishable benefits upon mankind."

The decline of religion

Bahá'u'lláh was also deeply concerned about the corruption and abuse of religion that had come to characterize human societies around the planet. He warned of the inevitable decline of religion's influence in the spheres of decision making and on the human heart. This decline, He explained, sets in when the noble and pure teachings of the moral luminaries Who founded the world's great religions are corrupted by selfish human ideas, superstition, and the worldly quest for power. "Should the lamp of religion be obscured," explained

Bahá'u'lláh, "chaos and confusion will ensue, and the lights of fairness and justice, of tranquility and peace cease to shine."

From the perspective of the Bahá'í teachings, the abuses carried out in the name of religion and the various forms of prejudice, superstition, dogma, exclusivity, and irrationality that have become entrenched in religious thought and practice prevent religion from bringing to bear the healing influence and society-building power it possesses.

Beyond these manifestations of the corruption of religion are the acts of terror and violence heinously carried out in, of all things, the name of God. Such acts have left a grotesque scar on the consciousness of humanity and distorted the concept of religion in the minds of countless people, turning many away from it altogether.

The spiritual and moral void resulting from the decline of religion has not only given rise to virulent forms of religious fanaticism, but has also allowed for a materialistic

conception of life to become the world's dominant paradigm.

Religion's place as an authority and a guiding light both in the public sphere and in the private lives of individuals has undergone a profound decline in the last century. A compelling assumption has become consolidated: as societies become more civilized, religion's role in humanity's collective affairs diminishes and is relegated to the private life of the individual. Ultimately, some have speculated that religion will disappear altogether.

Yet this assumption is not holding up in the light of recent developments. In these first decades of the 21st century, religion has experienced a resurgence as a social force of global importance. In a rapidly changing world, a reawakening of humanity's longing for meaning and for spiritual connection is finding expression in various forms: in the efforts of established faiths to meet the needs of rising generations by reshaping doctrines and practices to adapt to contemporary life; in interfaith activities that seek to foster dialogue between religious groups; in a myriad of spiritual movements, often focused on individual fulfillment and personal development; but also in the rise of fundamentalism and radical expressions of religious practice, which have tragically exploited the growing discontent among segments of humanity, especially youth.

Concurrently, national and international governing institutions are not only recognizing religion's enduring presence in society but are increasingly seeing the value of its participation in efforts to address humanity's most vexing problems. This realization has led to increased efforts to engage religious leaders and communities in decision making and in the carrying out of various plans and programs for social betterment.

"Should the lamp of religion be obscured, chaos and confusion will ensue, and the lights of fairness and justice, of tranquility and peace cease to shine."

—BAHÁ'U'LLÁH

"O people! Consort with the followers of all religions in a spirit of friendliness and fellowship."

— BAHÁ'U'LLÁH

Each of these expressions, however, falls far short of acknowledging the importance of a social force that has time and again demonstrated its power to inspire the building of vibrant civilizations. If religion is to exert its vital influence in this period of profound, often tumultuous change, it will need to be understood anew. Humanity will have to shed harmful conceptions and practices that masquerade as religion. The question is how to understand religion in the modern world and allow for its constructive powers to be released for the betterment of all.

Religion renewed

The great religious systems that have guided humanity over thousands of years can be regarded in essence as one unfolding religion that has been renewed from age to age, evolving as humanity has moved from one stage of collective development to another. Religion can thus be seen as a system of knowledge and practice that has, together with science, propelled the advancement of civilization throughout history.

Religion today cannot be exactly what it was in a previous era. Much of what is regarded as religion in the contemporary world must, Bahá'ís believe, be re-examined in light of the fundamental truths Bahá'u'lláh has posited: the oneness of God, the oneness of religion, and the oneness of the human family.

Bahá'u'lláh set an uncompromising standard: if religion becomes a source of separation, estrangement, or disagreement—much less violence and terror—it is best to do without it. The test of true religion is its fruits. Religion should demonstrably uplift humanity, create unity, forge good character, promote the search for truth, liberate human conscience, advance social justice, and promote the betterment of the world. True religion provides the moral foundations to harmonize relationships among individuals, communities, and institutions across diverse and complex social settings. It fosters an upright character and instills forbearance, compassion, forgiveness, magnanimity, and high-mindedness. It prohibits harm to others and invites souls to the plane of sacrifice, that they may give of themselves for the good of others. It imparts a world-embracing vision and cleanses the heart from self-centeredness and prejudice. It inspires souls to endeavor for material and spiritual betterment for all, to see their own happiness in that of others, to advance learning and science, to be an instrument of true joy, and to revive the body of humankind.

True religion is in harmony with science. When understood as complementary, science and religion provide people with powerful means to gain new and wondrous insights into reality and to shape the world around them, and each system benefits from an appropriate degree of influence from the other. Science, when devoid of the perspective of religion, can become vulnerable to dogmatic materialism. Religion, when devoid of science, falls prey to superstition and blind imitation of the past. The Bahá'í teachings state:

Put all your beliefs into harmony with science; there can be no opposition, for truth is one. When religion, shorn of its superstitions, traditions, and unintelligent dogmas, shows its conformity with science, then will there be a great unifying, cleansing force in the world which will sweep before it all wars, disagreements, discords and struggles— and then will mankind be united in the power of the Love of God.

True religion transforms the human heart and contributes to the transformation of society. It provides insights about humanity's true nature and the principles upon which civilization can advance. At this critical juncture in human history, the foundational spiritual principle of our time is the oneness of humankind. This simple statement represents a profound truth that, once accepted, invalidates all past notions of the superiority of any race, sex, or nationality. It is more than a mere call to mutual respect and feelings of goodwill between the diverse peoples of the world, important as these are. Carried to its logical conclusion, it implies an organic change in the very structure of society and in the relationships that sustain it.

The experience of the Bahá'í community

Inspired by the principle of the oneness of humankind, Bahá'ís believe that the advancement of a materially and spiritually coherent world civilization will require the contributions of countless high-minded individuals, groups, and organizations, for generations to come. The efforts of the Bahá'í community to contribute to this movement are finding expression today in localities all around the world and are open to all.

At the heart of Bahá'í endeavors is a long-term process of community building that seeks to develop patterns of life and social structures founded on the oneness of humanity. One component of these efforts is an educational process that has developed organically in rural and urban settings around the world. Spaces are created for children, youth, and adults to explore spiritual concepts and gain capacity to apply them to their own social environments. Every soul is invited to contribute regardless of race, gender, or creed. As thousands upon thousands participate, they draw insights from both science and the world's spiritual heritage and contribute to the development of new knowledge. Over time, capacities for service are being cultivated in diverse settings around the world and are giving rise to individual initiatives and increasingly complex collective action for the betterment of society. Transformation of the individual and transformation of the community unfold simultaneously.

Beyond efforts to learn about community building at the grass roots, Bahá'ís engage in various forms of social action, through which they strive to apply spiritual principles in efforts to further material progress in diverse settings. Bahá'í institutions and agencies, as well as individuals and organizations, also participate in the prevalent discourses of their societies in diverse spaces, from academic and professional settings, to national and international forums, all with the aim of contributing to the advancement of society.

As they carry out this work, Bahá'ís are conscious that to uphold high ideals is not the same as to embody them. The Bahá'í community recognizes that many challenges lie ahead as it works shoulder to shoulder with others for unity and justice. It is committed to the long-term process of learning through action that this task entails, with the conviction that religion has a vital role to play in society and a unique power to release the potential of individuals, communities, and institutions. ❂

"Be anxiously concerned with the needs of the age ye live in, and center your deliberations on its exigencies and requirements."

— BAHÁ'U'LLÁH

ONE GOD

Called by different names throughout the ages, the eternal God, the Creator of the universe, is limitless, all-knowing, all-powerful, and all-loving. God is one. The reality of God is beyond human understanding, though we may find expressions of God's attributes in every created thing.

"The peoples of the world, of whatever race or religion, derive their inspiration from one heavenly Source, and are the subjects of one God."

—BAHÁ'U'LLÁH

"This is the changeless Faith of God, eternal in the past, eternal in the future."

—BAHÁ'U'LLÁH

ONE UNFOLDING RELIGION

Humanity's spiritual, intellectual, and moral capacities have been cultivated through the successive teachings of the Founders of the world's religions—the Manifestations of God. Among Them are Krishna, Abraham, Moses, Zoroaster, Buddha, Jesus Christ, Muhammad, and, most recently, the Báb and Bahá'u'lláh. Each religion originates with God and is suited to the age and place in which it is revealed. In essence, the religion of God is one and is progressively unfolding.

"Ye are the fruits of one tree, and the leaves of one branch. Deal ye one with another with the utmost love and harmony, with friendliness and fellowship."

—BAHÁ'U'LLÁH

ONE HUMAN FAMILY

Beyond all differences of race, culture, class, or ethnicity, regardless of differences in customs, opinions, or temperaments, every individual is a member of one gloriously diverse human family. Each unique individual has a role to play in carrying forward an ever-advancing material and spiritual civilization.

AT A GLANCE

Origins

The Bahá'í Faith was born in Persia (today Iran) in the mid-19th century. In less than 200 years it has become a universal faith present in every country in the world with adherents from virtually every national, ethnic, religious, and tribal background.

Founders

The Bahá'í Faith originated with **Bahá'u'lláh** (1817-1892), Whose title means "the Glory of God." Bahá'ís regard Him as the latest in the succession of Divine Messengers Who founded the world's major religions. He is the Promised One They foretold. In His writings, Bahá'u'lláh outlines a framework for the development of a global civilization which takes into account both the spiritual and material dimensions of human life. His teachings, centered around the recognition of the oneness of humanity, offer a compelling vision of an approaching world united in justice, peace, and prosperity.

Bahá'u'lláh's coming was heralded by the **Báb** (1819-1850), meaning "the Gate." The Báb proclaimed His divine mission in 1844, which is considered the beginning of the Bahá'í Era—a new cycle of human history and social evolution.

A movement of personal and social transformation

The millions worldwide who constitute the international Bahá'í community are quite possibly the most diverse organized body of people on the planet. United by their belief in Bahá'u'lláh, and inspired by His teachings, members strive to live out the twofold moral purpose of transforming their own characters while contributing to the advancement of society.

Sacred writings

The writings of the Báb and Bahá'u'lláh are considered by Bahá'ís to have been revealed by God. As the creative Word of God, these sacred writings have the power to touch the deepest recesses of our hearts and transform us and the world around us. The Bahá'í writings address the needs of the age and offer inspiration for individuals working to better themselves and their communities. Bahá'u'lláh enjoined His followers to read daily from the sacred texts: *"Immerse yourselves in the ocean of My words, that ye may unravel its secrets, and discover all the pearls of wisdom that lie hid in its depths."*

Worship

Daily prayer, offered both in private and in the company of others, is regarded by Bahá'ís as essential spiritual nourishment, providing inspiration for positive personal and social change. Bahá'ís consider work done in the spirit of service to humanity as the highest form of worship. Individuals pray daily and observe an annual 19-day period of fasting during daylight hours. The Bahá'í Faith has no clergy or sacraments, and has simple practices for life's rites of passage, such as marriage and funerals.

Structure

The affairs of the Bahá'í community are governed by institutions established by Bahá'u'lláh. This Administrative Order comprises both elected and appointed institutions at local, national, and international levels. Nonpartisan elections, without nominations or campaigns and conducted by secret ballot, and collective decision making are hallmarks of Bahá'í administration. These and other principles constitute a model of just and unified global governance.

ONE
HUMAN FAMILY

The conviction that every individual belongs to one human family is at the heart of the Bahá'í Faith. We are all citizens and co-stewards of one planet. A growing awareness of our common heritage and interdependence allows us to strive for unity in our diversity. The Bahá'í writings assert that we are "flowers of one garden, leaves of one tree" and share a common purpose—to carry forward an ever-advancing material and spiritual civilization. Bahá'u'lláh proclaimed the oneness of humanity and called for the removal of any cause of division that would lead people to see themselves as "us" and "them."

"Humanity may be likened unto the vari-colored flowers of one garden. There is unity in diversity. Each sets off and enhances the other's beauty."

— 'ABDU'L-BAHÁ

Oneness of humanity and elimination of prejudice

The principle of the oneness of humankind is the central teaching of the Bahá'í Faith. Recognition and acceptance of this principle necessitates the abandonment of prejudice of every kind—race, class, color, gender, creed, nationality, age, material wealth—everything that people have used to consider themselves superior or inferior to others. Indeed, Bahá'u'lláh's vision for a new civilization inspires people to see themselves as citizens of one common homeland, which is the planet itself.

Prejudice—false perception—blinds us to the fact that every person is essentially a spiritual being with unique talents and capacities, a "mine rich in gems of inestimable value."

Bahá'u'lláh compared the world of humanity to the human body. Healthy functioning of the body depends on cooperation. Millions of cells, diverse in form and function, play their part in maintaining health. The body's various parts do not compete for resources; rather, each cell plays its role in a continuous process of giving and receiving. So it is with individual humans in an interconnected world.

Genuine, universal fellowship is a requisite for realizing human unity. According to the Bahá'í writings, "So intense must be the spirit of love and loving kindness, that the stranger may find himself a friend, the enemy a true brother, no difference whatsoever existing between them."

Truly putting into practice the principle of the oneness of humankind, however, goes beyond overcoming prejudice and awakening the spirit of brotherhood and goodwill. The Bahá'í writings state that "It implies an organic change in the structure of present-day society, a change such as the world has not yet experienced....It calls for no less than the reconstruction and demilitarization" of the planet, for a "world organically unified in all the essential

The Bahá'í Guaymi Cultural Center serves a significant population of Guaymi Bahá'ís in the province of Chiriqui, Panama. The Guaymi are one of more than 2,000 tribes represented in the Bahá'í Faith.

aspects of its life" and yet infinite in its diversity. The writings affirm that attainment of this stage of human evolution "is not only necessary but inevitable."

A commitment to selfless service

A natural expression of the love of God and the acceptance of the principle of the oneness of humanity is selfless service to our fellow human beings. "Man's merit lieth

in service and virtue and not in the pageantry of wealth and riches," wrote Bahá'u'lláh. "The betterment of the world can be accomplished through pure and goodly deeds, through commendable and seemly conduct."

Bahá'u'lláh's son, 'Abdu'l-Bahá, wrote:

And the honor and distinction of the individual consist in this, that he among all the world's multitudes should become a source of social good. Is any larger bounty conceivable than this, that an individual, looking within himself, should find that by the confirming grace of God he has become the cause of peace and well-being, of happiness and advantage to his fellow men? No, by the one true God, there is no greater bliss, no more complete delight. ●

In less than 200 years, the Bahá'í Faith has become a universal faith present in every country of the world. It is quite possibly the most diverse organized body of people on the planet.

BAHÁ'U'LLÁH
and the DAWN OF A NEW DAY

The Bahá'í writings often compare the coming of a Manifestation of God to the rising of the sun. The appearance of God's Messenger is like the start of each new day, when the sun's rays release energy into the world, shedding light on all things and allowing the eye to see what was obscure in the darkness of night.

Dawn over Bahjí, in northern Israel, where the Shrine of Bahá'u'lláh is located.

A new day has dawned for humanity with the coming of Bahá'u'lláh and His Herald, the Báb—the two most recent of the Divine Messengers Who have appeared throughout history. Just as the dawning sun stirs the sleeping world to life, the rising of these Twin Manifestations of God has re-energized humanity's search for higher meaning and purpose in life. Bahá'u'lláh's teachings shed light on human affairs at a time when, it can be argued, darkness has settled on the world. His teachings help humanity make sense of and navigate the great changes that are rapidly unfolding. While these changes disrupt the order of things, create chaos, and perplex even the most astute leaders, they also open the way for new patterns of life and new forms of human organization to emerge.

In this turbulent period of human history, the world is in need of a unifying vision of our true nature as human beings and of the kind of world in which we would want to live. Bahá'ís believe that this vision is revealed in the writings of Bahá'u'lláh, Whose life and teachings are the most compelling story of our time. Born in Persia (modern Iran) in 1817, Bahá'u'lláh established a Cause that has gradually captured the imagination and dedication of millions of people from virtually every race, culture, class, and nation on earth.

Bahá'u'lláh's writings not only affirm that human nature is fundamentally spiritual, but go further to proclaim that our development as individuals is intimately connected to the advancement of our

communities and ultimately of our societies. Worship of God and service to humanity are two inseparable aspects of life, enabling both individuals and society to progress.

Bahá'u'lláh's teachings cover a vast range of subjects, from social issues such as racial justice, the equality of the sexes, and wealth inequity to those innermost questions that affect the life of the soul. The original texts, many of them written in His own hand, have been meticulously preserved. For over a century and a half, individuals, communities, and institutions have been striving to realize the wondrous vision of peace and unity presented in His writings.

Bahá'u'lláh's coming was heralded by the Báb, a young merchant from Shiraz, Persia, Who proclaimed in 1844 that He was the bearer of a new message from God and the harbinger of the Promised One of all religions. The following sections explore the lives of these Twin Manifestations Who are regarded as the Founders of the Bahá'í Faith.

"All praise be to Thee, O my God, inasmuch as Thou hast adorned the world with the splendor of the dawn following the night."

— BAHÁ'U'LLÁH

THE BAHÁ'ÍS

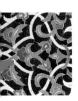

The Báb
Herald of the Bahá'í Faith

"Is there any Remover of difficulties save God? Say: Praised be God! He is God! All are His servants and all abide by His bidding!"

—THE BÁB

The Bahá'í Faith has its roots in Persia. In the mid-1800s, when countries in Europe and North America were beginning a period of unprecedented technological, material, and political advancement, this once-glorious land was mired in political and religious corruption.

This was a time of great religious expectation. Predictions by Bible scholars sparked a wave of Adventist movements in the United States and Europe. In the Middle East, scholars of Islam eagerly spread the word that the "day of the return" foretold in the Qur'án was at hand. Other faiths and traditions around the world had long anticipated the appearance of a Promised One.

In 1844, in Shiraz, Persia, a young merchant, Siyyid 'Alí-Muhammad, referring to Himself as the Báb, meaning "the Gate," proclaimed that He was the bearer of a new revelation from God. The Báb called for people to seek truth for themselves and prepare for "Him Whom God shall make manifest," another Divine Messenger, greater than Himself, Who would soon appear to guide humanity towards global justice, unity, and peace.

The Báb wrote extensively. He composed eloquent prayers and profound expositions and commentaries, many of which spoke of the coming Divine Teacher. He was an advocate of the poor. He called for the advancement of women and encouraged universal education and the study of science—radical ideas at the time, in a stifling society oppressed by fanatical religious orthodoxy.

Perceiving this progressive new Faith as a threat, religious and civil authorities in Persia imprisoned the Báb and tortured, imprisoned, and killed thousands of His followers, setting a precedent for waves of religious persecution of the Bahá'ís that continue to the present day. Despite all attempts at repression, however, the movement spread like wildfire.

One of the Báb's most courageous followers was the poet, Táhirih, who sought to transcend restrictions placed on her as a woman in a traditional society. She gave her life for the cause of the Báb. "You can kill me as soon as you like," Táhirih told her assassins, "but you cannot stop the emancipation of women."

Qazvin province in north Iran

In 1850, the Báb's six-year ministry was cut short when He was executed by firing squad in a public square in Tabriz. The light the Báb had lit in the land was not so easily extinguished, however. His followers persevered. The shattered remains of the Báb's body were rescued and moved from place to place by His followers for nearly 60 years until they could be fittingly laid to rest.

The barrack-square in Tabriz, Persia, where the Báb was martyred in 1850.

Illuminated Tablet of the Báb

1844

The Báb is not only a Forerunner or Herald, but a Manifestation of God in His own right. Bahá'ís consider the year 1844, when the Báb first made His declaration, as the beginning of the Bahá'í Era—a new cycle of human history and social evolution.

SELECTION OF WRITINGS FROM THE BÁB

On God's bond with creation

God hath, at all times and under all conditions, been wholly independent of His creatures. He hath cherished and will ever cherish the desire that all men may attain His gardens of Paradise with utmost love, that no one should sadden another, not even for a moment, and that all should dwell within His cradle of protection and security until the Day of Resurrection which marketh the dayspring of the Revelation of Him Whom God will make manifest.

On our soul's aspiration

There is no paradise more wondrous for any soul than to be exposed to God's Manifestation in His Day, to hear His verses and believe in them, to attain His presence, which is naught but the presence of God, to sail upon the sea of the heavenly kingdom of His good-pleasure, and to partake of the choice fruits of the paradise of His divine Oneness.

Prayer for reliance on God

O my God, my Lord and my Master! I have detached myself from my kindred and have sought through Thee to become independent of all that dwell on earth and ever ready to receive that which is praiseworthy in Thy sight. Bestow on me such good as will make me independent of aught else but Thee, and grant me an ampler share of Thy boundless favors. Verily, Thou art the Lord of grace abounding.

Prayer for trusting God

O Lord! Unto Thee I repair for refuge, and toward all Thy signs I set my heart.

O Lord! Whether traveling or at home, and in my occupation or in my work, I place my whole trust in Thee.

Grant me then Thy sufficing help so as to make me independent of all things, O Thou Who art unsurpassed in Thy mercy!

Bestow upon me my portion, O Lord, as Thou pleasest, and cause me to be satisfied with whatsoever Thou hast ordained for me.

Thine is the absolute authority to command.

The house of the Báb in Shiraz, Iran, where He declared His mission in 1844. The building was destroyed by the Iranian government in 1979.

Door of the Shrine of the Báb in Haifa, Israel

The Shrine of the Báb

The Shrine of the Báb is a singular point of attraction on the northern slope of Mount Carmel in the port city of Haifa, Israel. The building's gold-tiled dome and harmonious blend of Eastern and Western architectural styles have made it a familiar and well-loved landmark on the Mediterranean coast. This luminous structure, in which the Báb's earthly remains are buried, is surrounded by 19 terraces of lush gardens. For members of the Bahá'í Faith, it is one of the holiest places in the world.

Bahá'u'lláh

The Divine Educator for this day

Bahá'u'lláh, "the Glory of God," is the Promised One foretold by the Báb and by the Divine Messengers of the past. His teachings affirm humanity's eternal relationship with the Divine and provide a vision of the future which has inspired millions from every part of the planet and every walk of life.

Bahá'u'lláh delivered a new revelation from God. His mission was to spiritually re-awaken humanity and unite all the peoples of the world. Bahá'u'lláh's teachings form the basis of the Bahá'í Faith and offer a vision of infinite hope and healing for the world.

In His writings, Bahá'u'lláh outlines a framework for the development of a global civilization that takes into account both the spiritual and material dimensions of human life. He offers a vision of a world where the recognition of the oneness of humanity ultimately leads to lasting justice, peace, and prosperity.

"My object is none other than the betterment of the world and the tranquility of its peoples," wrote Bahá'u'lláh. For this noble purpose, He endured a life of persecution, imprisonment, torture, and exile.

Illuminated Tablet
of Bahá'u'lláh

Bahá'u'lláh's imprisonment began in Persia in 1852 when, as a supporter of the Báb, He was arrested, tortured, and cast into a subterranean dungeon, Tehran's notorious Síyáh-Chál, the "Black Pit."

It was during this imprisonment, through the foul prison air, filth, and pitch-black darkness, that the first stirrings of a divine revelation came to Him. As Bahá'u'lláh sat with His feet in stocks and a 100-pound iron chain around His neck, the Holy Spirit of God was revealed to Him.

This was an event comparable to those great moments of the ancient past when God revealed Himself to His earlier Messengers: when Moses stood before the Burning Bush; when the Buddha received enlightenment under the Bodhi tree; when the Holy

Spirit, in the form of a dove, descended upon Jesus; and when the angel Gabriel appeared to Muhammad.

In His writings, Bahá'u'lláh later described the experience and the essence of God's revelation coming through Him:

The breezes of the All-Glorious were wafted over Me, and taught Me the knowledge of all that hath been. This thing is not from Me, but from One Who is Almighty and All-Knowing. And He bade Me lift up My voice between earth and heaven....

"Bahá'u'lláh's teachings...now present us with the highest and purest form of religious teaching."

—LEO TOLSTOY, RUSSIAN AUTHOR

ADRIANOPLE

CONSTANTINOPLE

The house of Rida Big, where
Bahá'u'lláh stayed in Adrianople.

Exterior of the prison cell
where Bahá'u'lláh was first
confined in 'Akká.

Map showing
the route of
Bahá'u'lláh's
exiles

OTTOMAN
EMPIRE

PERSIA

*During the days I lay in the prison of
Tihrán, though the galling weight of the
chains and the stench-filled air allowed
Me but little sleep, still in those infrequent
moments of slumber I felt as if something
flowed from the crown of My head over
My breast, even as a mighty torrent that
precipitateth itself upon the earth from
the summit of a lofty mountain. Every
limb of My body would, as a result, be
set afire. At such moments My tongue
recited what no man could bear to hear.*

Upon His release from the Black Pit,
Bahá'u'lláh was banished from His home-
land in what began 40 years of exile,
the remainder of His earthly life. He publicly
announced His mission as God's
Messenger in 1863.

The followers of Bahá'u'lláh became known
as Bahá'ís. As these followers multiplied,
attracted by His magnetic character and
deeply spiritual teachings, Bahá'u'lláh
was further exiled. He was sentenced to
imprisonment in the harshest penal colony
in the Ottoman Empire, the ancient city
of 'Akká, located in what is now Israel.
The foul climate, lack of fresh water, and
vermin-infested buildings made life in 'Akká
one of the most severe punishments possible.
Bahá'u'lláh arrived there in 1868, along with
70 of His family members and followers.

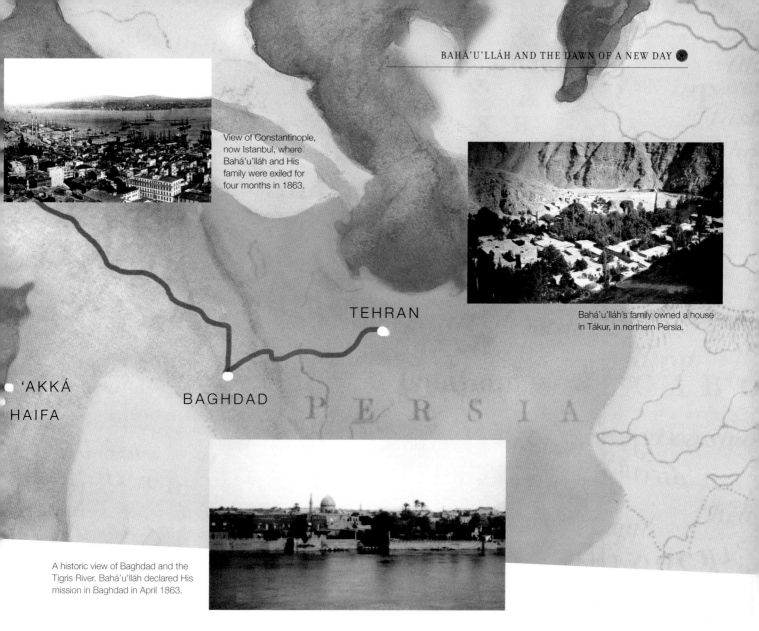

View of Constantinople, now Istanbul, where Bahá'u'lláh and His family were exiled for four months in 1863.

Bahá'u'lláh's family owned a house in Tákur, in northern Persia.

TEHRAN

'AKKÁ

HAIFA

BAGHDAD

PERSIA

A historic view of Baghdad and the Tigris River. Bahá'u'lláh declared His mission in Baghdad in April 1863.

It was in 'Akká that Bahá'u'lláh wrote some of His most important works, addressing the kings and rulers of His day, and revealing the laws and principles that would lead humanity into an era of universal peace. "The earth is but one country and mankind its citizens," He wrote. "It is not for him to pride himself who loveth his own country, but rather for him who loveth the whole world."

As time passed, local authorities relaxed the conditions of Bahá'u'lláh's imprisonment and He moved a short distance north to Bahjí, where He spent the last 12 years of His life. During this period, Bahá'u'lláh made several visits to the nearby slopes of Mount Carmel where, in 1891, He designated a permanent resting place for the remains of His Forerunner, the Báb.

In 1892, after a brief illness, Bahá'u'lláh passed from this life at the age of 75. His earthly remains were laid to rest in a small building next to His final residence in Bahjí. The burial sites of the Báb and Bahá'u'lláh have become sacred shrines and places of pilgrimage for Bahá'ís from around the world, who visit them to draw spiritual strength and inspiration, and to dedicate themselves to the work of creating the transformed world Bahá'u'lláh envisioned. ◉

"The Ancient Beauty hath consented to be bound with chains that mankind may be released from its bondage."

—BAHÁ'U'LLÁH

The house of Bahá'u'lláh in Tákur, northern Iran, destroyed by the Iranian government in 1981.

BAHÁ'U'LLÁH'S EARLY LIFE

Bahá'u'lláh was born in Tehran on November 12, 1817, and was named Mírzá Husayn-'Alí. His father, Mírzá Buzurg, held a high-ranking position in the court of the Persian king.

At a young age, Bahá'u'lláh exhibited qualities that made those around Him realize He was no ordinary child. He possessed an innate wisdom and intelligence, even though He did not attend school, and as He grew, the signs of His greatness became increasingly clear.

Bahá'u'lláh became known for His keen insight, His excellent character, His generosity and compassion. At the age of 18, Bahá'u'lláh married a young woman, Navváb, and their home became a shelter, a place of light and love and hospitality, open to all.

Bahá'u'lláh was 22 years old when His father passed away, leaving Him responsible for managing the household and extensive family estates. The government offered Bahá'u'lláh His father's ministerial post, but He declined this prominent position. He was not interested in titles and honors; His interest was in defending and protecting the poor and the needy. Instead of pursuing a life of power and leisure, Bahá'u'lláh chose to devote His energies to charity and acts of service. By the early 1840s, He had become known as "Father of the Poor."

With Bahá'u'lláh's acceptance of the religion of the Báb in 1844, life permanently changed for the young nobleman and His family. Although Bahá'u'lláh and the Báb never met in person, they corresponded. From the moment Bahá'u'lláh heard of the Báb's message, He declared His wholehearted belief in the cause and put all of His energy and influence into promoting it.

Top: Entrance to the house of Bahá'u'lláh in Tákur

Bottom: A garden at Bahá'u'lláh's house in Shimran. Bahá'u'lláh loved nature and spent much of His time in the outdoors. He remarked, "The country is the world of the soul, the city is the world of bodies."

The writings of Bahá'u'lláh

As the Torah is to Jews, the Gospel to Christians, and the Qur'án to Muslims, the writings of Bahá'u'lláh are considered by Bahá'ís to be the revealed Word of God. Bahá'u'lláh's collected works of more than 100 volumes form the foundation of Bahá'í sacred scripture.

Bahá'u'lláh wrote in both Arabic and Persian, showing superb mastery of both languages. Some works speak with the voice of God in lofty and beautiful prose. Some are direct statements on morality and ethics, while others are prayers, meditations, and mystical works. Many are letters to individuals, called "Tablets."

Foremost among Bahá'u'lláh's writings is the Kitáb-i-Aqdas (The Most Holy Book). This book of laws and ordinances, revealed during the darkest days of His imprisonment, contains the guidance and prescriptions that lead to personal happiness and peaceful society.

A small book of passages revealed by Bahá'u'lláh entitled the Hidden Words conveys the essence of His ethical teachings. It is a distillation of spiritual guidance contained in the sacred texts of the world's religions.

O SON OF SPIRIT!
My first counsel is this:
Possess a pure, kindly and radiant heart, that thine may be a sovereignty ancient, imperishable and everlasting.

In the Kitáb-i-Íqán (The Book of Certitude), Bahá'u'lláh explains the continuity of revealed religion through the ages. He addresses themes that have always been central to religious life: the existence of God, the station of God's Messengers, the nature of humanity, and the purpose of life.

The best known of Bahá'u'lláh's mystical writings is the Seven Valleys. In poetic language, it traces the stages of the soul's journey to union with its Creator.

The process of translating the sacred writings of the Bahá'í Faith is ongoing. The standard for translation into English was established by Shoghi Effendi, Bahá'u'lláh's great-grandson, who headed the Faith from 1921 to 1957. His translations reflect a brilliant command of the English language and an authoritative understanding of the texts.

Illuminated manuscript from the Kitáb-i-Aqdas (The Most Holy Book) by Bahá'u'lláh

MAJOR PUBLISHED WORKS OF BAHÁ'U'LLÁH

Kitáb-i-Aqdas
The Most Holy Book

Kitáb-i-Íqán
The Book of Certitude

The Hidden Words

Gleanings from the Writings of Bahá'u'lláh

Prayers and Meditations by Bahá'u'lláh

The Seven Valleys and the Four Valleys

Epistle to the Son of the Wolf

The Summons of the Lord of Hosts

Gems of Divine Mysteries

The Tabernacle of Unity

THE SHRINE OF BAHÁ'U'LLÁH

Bahá'u'lláh was residing in the Mansion of Bahjí in Akká when He passed from this life in 1892. His remains were laid to rest in a small adjacent building, now a Shrine of striking simplicity and beauty. The tranquility and sanctity of the site are enhanced by the surrounding gardens which include ancient fig, olive, and cypress groves.

The Shrine of Bahá'u'lláh is the holiest place on earth for Bahá'ís. This is the spot towards which they turn each day in prayer. Pilgrims visit this Shrine from all corners of the globe to pay their respects to Bahá'u'lláh and to dedicate their lives to the noble purposes that He set before humanity.

Page from the Epistle to the
Son of the Wolf in the handwriting
of Bahá'u'lláh's secretary

Documenting the Word of God

One significant feature of Bahá'u'lláh's writings is their authenticity. For the first time in religious history, the words of a Manifestation of God were recorded and authenticated at the time they were revealed.

This process of revelation—the act of bringing forth the Word of God—is described in several historical documents. One observer recorded the following:

Mírzá Áqá Ján (Bahá'u'lláh's personal secretary) had a large inkpot the size of a small bowl. He also had available about ten to twelve pens and large sheets of paper in stacks. In those days all letters which arrived for Bahá'u'lláh were received by Mírzá Áqá Ján. He would bring these into the presence of Bahá'u'lláh, and after having obtained permission, would read them. After-wards [Bahá'u'lláh] would direct him to take up his pen and record the Tablet which was revealed in reply.

Such was the speed with which he used to write the revealed Word that the ink of the first words was scarcely yet dry when the whole page was finished. It seemed as if someone had dipped a lock of hair in the ink and applied it over the whole page.

—Eyewitness to how the words of Bahá'u'lláh were recorded

Cut-reed pen and ink spoon
used by Bahá'u'lláh

After each period of revelation, the original manuscript would be re-transcribed, with Bahá'u'lláh Himself overseeing and approving the final version.

Selection of writings from Bahá'u'lláh

On humanity's relationship to God

Veiled in My immemorial being and in the ancient eternity of My essence, I knew My love for thee; therefore I created thee, have engraved on thee Mine image and revealed to thee My beauty.

On knowing God

The door of the knowledge of the Ancient Being hath ever been, and will continue forever to be, closed in the face of men. No man's understanding shall ever gain access unto His holy court. As a token of His mercy, however, and as a proof of His loving-kindness, He hath manifested unto men the Daystars of His divine guidance, the Symbols of His divine unity, and hath ordained the knowledge of these sanctified Beings to be identical with the knowledge of His own Self.... They are the Manifestations of God amidst men, the evidences of His Truth, and the signs of His glory.

On life's purpose

The whole duty of man in this Day is to attain that share of the flood of grace which God poureth forth for him. Let none, therefore, consider the largeness or smallness of the receptacle. The portion of some might lie in the palm of a man's hand, the portion of others might fill a cup, and of others even a gallon-measure.

On our creation

Know ye not why We created you all from the same dust? That no one should exalt himself over the other. Ponder at all times in your hearts how ye were created. Since We have created you all from one same substance it is incumbent on you to be even as one soul, to walk with the same feet, eat with the same mouth and dwell in the same land, that from your inmost being, by your deeds and actions, the signs of oneness and the essence of detachment may be made manifest. Such is My counsel to you, O concourse of light! Heed ye this counsel that ye may obtain the fruit of holiness from the tree of wondrous glory.

On prayer

Intone, O my servant, the verses of God that have been received by thee, as intoned by them who have drawn nigh unto Him, that the sweetness of thy melody may kindle thine own soul, and attract the hearts of all men. Whoso reciteth, in the privacy of his chamber, the verses revealed by God, the scattering angels of the Almighty shall scatter abroad the fragrance of the words uttered by his mouth, and shall cause the heart of every righteous man to throb. Though he may, at first, remain unaware of its effect, yet the virtue of the grace vouchsafed unto him must needs sooner or later exercise its influence upon his soul. Thus have the mysteries of the Revelation of God been decreed by virtue of the Will of Him Who is the Source of power and wisdom.

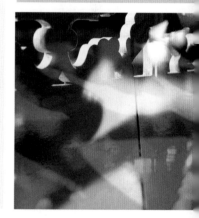

On an ever-advancing civilization

The betterment of the world can be accomplished through pure and goodly deeds, through commendable and seemly conduct.

WHAT BAHÁ'ÍS BELIEVE

Bahá'u'lláh taught the oneness of God and religion, the oneness of humanity and freedom from prejudice, the inherent nobility of the human being, the progressive revelation of religious truth, the development of spiritual qualities, and the integration of worship and service.

The Bahá'í writings also address the fundamental equality of the sexes, the harmony between religion and science, the need to eliminate extremes of wealth and poverty, the centrality of justice to all human endeavors, the importance of education, and the dynamics of the relationships that are to bind together individuals, communities, and institutions as humanity advances towards its collective maturity.

"Immerse yourselves in the ocean of My words, that ye may unravel its secrets, and discover all the pearls of wisdom that lie hid in its depths."

— BAHÁ'U'LLÁH

"The peoples of the world, of whatever race or religion, derive their inspiration from one heavenly Source, and are the subjects of one God."

— BAHÁ'U'LLÁH

One loving Creator

The Bahá'í writings explain that although we may find expression of God's attributes in every created thing, although we can see signs of God in the beauty, richness, and diversity of the natural world, the reality of God—as Creator of the universe and all that is in it—is beyond the understanding of any mortal mind. God is limitless, infinite, and all-powerful. God is all-knowing, all-merciful, and all-loving. God is one.

Out of love for humanity, God has revealed Himself and His Will through a series of Divine Messengers, or "Manifestations of God." What we know about the unknowable God has been taught to us by these successive Founders of the world's religions. Their teachings help us develop and express our spiritual attributes and draw closer to our Creator.

Although the exact nature of God eludes us, the purpose of our lives is to recognize, love, and grow closer to Him. We may do so by striving to emulate God's attributes, such as love, compassion, generosity, justice, and mercy, in both our inner lives and our actions.

One human family

The conviction that we belong to a single human family is at the heart of the Bahá'í Faith. The principle of the oneness of humankind is the pivot around which all the teachings of Bahá'u'lláh revolve.

Misconceptions and prejudices that consider one group of people as superior to another are a major contributor to humanity's present afflictions. Racism retards the potentiality of its victims, corrupts its perpetrators, and blights human progress. If this problem is to be overcome, the oneness of humanity must be universally upheld and protected by law and through social policies and structures.

No ethnic or cultural grouping is superior to another. All receive God's love in equal measure. Recognition by the biological and social sciences that there is only one human "race" removes any basis for prejudice. Every individual, from whatever background, can contribute to the betterment of the world.

Love of all the world's peoples does not exclude love of one's country. But unbridled nationalism and its associated prejudices must give way to a wider loyalty, to the love of humanity as a whole. "Let not a man glory in that he loves his country," said Bahá'u'lláh, "let him rather glory in this, that he loves his kind."

Equality of the sexes

Another prerequisite for building a united world is the achievement of full equality between women and men. There are no grounds, moral, practical, or biological, upon which denial of the equality of the sexes can be justified. Gender prejudice perpetrates injustice against women and promotes harmful attitudes and habits in men that are carried from the family to the workplace, to economic and political life, and ultimately to relations among countries.

"God is the Shepherd of all and we are His flock. There are not many races. There is only one race."

— 'ABDU'L-BAHÁ

37

One unfolding religion

"This is the changeless Faith of God, eternal in the past, eternal in the future."

— BAHÁ'U'LLÁH

The religions of the world have been founded by the successive Manifestations of God. Each religion originates with God and is suited to the age and place in which it is revealed. In essence, the religion of God is one and is progressively unfolding.

Religions have the power to inspire breathtaking achievements in all fields of human endeavor and to elicit extraordinary qualities of heroism, self-sacrifice, and self-discipline from their followers. Religions produce universal codes of law and institutional systems that allow people to live together in ever-larger and more complex societies.

Throughout history, however, strife between religions has been the cause of innumerable wars and conflicts, and a major barrier to progress. The separations and conflicts between people, carried out in the name of religion, are contrary to its true nature and purpose. "If religion becomes a cause of dislike, hatred and division, it were better to be without it, and to withdraw from such a religion would be a truly religious act," said 'Abdu'l-Bahá. "Any religion which is not a cause of love and unity is no religion."

If all the great religions are from the same God, and can be considered to be one in essence, how can we understand their differences, particularly regarding social practices? Bahá'u'lláh explained that the Founders of the world's religions could be regarded as skilled physicians. Each has a central mission, and each has a complete grasp of the nature of the body of humanity and is able to prescribe the appropriate cures for the ills of the world at the time and place in which He appears.

The mission of Bahá'u'lláh, God's Messenger for this age, is to spiritually re-awaken and unite the peoples of the world. Bahá'u'lláh's teachings speak of peace as "the supreme goal of all mankind" and explain the spiritual principles that will guide humanity to this universal, lasting peace. This great peace has been promised by all of the previous Manifestations of God.

KRISHNA

ABRAHAM

MOSES

ZOROASTER

BUDDHA

5,000 YEARS AGO

4,000 YEARS AGO

3,000 YEARS AGO

Progressive revelation

If we liken God to the unapproachable blazing sun, then the Manifestations of God are like mirrors that perfectly reflect God's light to human beings.

Our knowledge of God, and humanity's spiritual, intellectual, and moral capacities, have been cultivated by these Manifestations of God. These Divine Educators appear in different places in the world at different times, with teachings essential for the development of the people in that place and time.

While each Manifestation has a distinct individuality and a definite mission, They all share a divinely ordained purpose—to educate all people, refine their character, and endue all created things with grace.

Though many of their names and teachings have been lost to history, we do know something of the lives and teachings of some of these Manifestations. Among them are Krishna, Abraham, Moses, Zoroaster,

Buddha, Jesus Christ, Muhammad, and, in more recent times, the Báb and Bahá'u'lláh.

With the coming of each Manifestation, spiritual forces are released which, over time, increasingly permeate human affairs, providing the main impulse for the further development of consciousness and society.

This process, in which the Manifestations of God have continuously provided the guidance necessary for humanity's social and spiritual evolution, is known as "progressive revelation." Bahá'u'lláh explicitly stated that after the passage of at least a thousand years, another Manifestation of God would appear.

"The Revelation of God may be likened to the sun. No matter how innumerable its risings, there is but one sun, and upon it depends the life of all things."

—THE BÁB

JESUS CHRIST

MUHAMMAD

THE BÁB

BAHÁ'U'LLÁH

2,000 YEARS AGO

1,000 YEARS AGO

TODAY

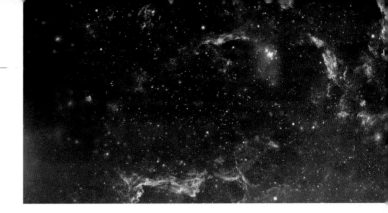

Harmony of religion and science

"Religion and science are the two wings upon which man's intelligence can soar into the heights, with which the human soul can progress."

—'ABDU'L-BAHÁ

One of the fundamental principles of the Bahá'í Faith is the harmony of science and religion. The Bahá'í teachings maintain that—just as science constitutes one vast, coherent system of knowledge that has evolved over centuries and millennia—there is at the deepest level one common religion, which is renewed from age to age, commensurate with humanity's social evolution. Together, science and religion constitute dual knowledge systems propelling civilization.

'Abdu'l-Bahá has described science as the "most noble" of all virtues and "the discoverer of all things." As an evolving system of knowledge, science has progressively enabled humanity to separate fact from conjecture and to gain ever greater insights into physical and social reality. Profound development of scientific capabilities—observing, measuring, rigorously testing ideas—have revolutionized human affairs, enabling us to construct a coherent understanding of the laws and processes governing the natural world. Scientific achievements have greatly accelerated over the past two centuries, leading to discoveries and technologies undreamt of only centuries before. Yet, devoid of the moral and ethical imperatives introduced by religion, science has become vulnerable to materialistic forces and interests that can direct its course toward base and destructive ends.

Throughout human history, religion has cultivated in countless people the capacity to love, to give generously, to serve others, to forgive, to trust in God, and to sacrifice for the common good. Whole civilizations have been founded upon the moral and spiritual insights that the great spiritual luminaries—the Manifestations of God—have brought to the world. In the final analysis, the impulses set in motion by these Founders of the world's religions have been the chief influence in the civilizing of human character.

According to the Bahá'í teachings, though, not everything referred to as religion is true to its name: true religion is a source of unity; true religion is in harmony with science. Devoid of scientific insights and rational thought, religion falls prey to superstition and blind imitation of the past, losing its vitalizing force. When this occurs, religion declines. Though different in nature from science, true religion, like science, advances and evolves over time. From the perspective of the Bahá'í teachings, this evolution occurs through the renewal of religion from age to age, with the coming of a new Manifestation of God. 'Abdu'l-Bahá said:

Note thou carefully that in this world of being, all things must ever be made new. Look at the material world about thee, see how it hath now been renewed. The thoughts have changed, the ways of life

have been revised, the sciences and arts show a new vigor, discoveries and inventions are new, perceptions are new. How then could such a vital power as religion—the guarantor of mankind's great advances, the very means of attaining everlasting life, the fosterer of infinite excellence, the light of both worlds—not be made new?

Bahá'ís believe that religion and science, as two knowledge systems, complement one another in efforts to bring about meaningful social transformation and to solve many of the vexing problems that plague humanity today. Around the world, Bahá'í communities are learning how knowledge about spiritual reality can find practical expression. Together with insights from science, such knowledge raises the capacity of individuals, institutions, and communities to become effective protagonists in the advancement of civilization.

The Bahá'í writings assert that, when the material and spiritual dimensions of the life of a community are kept in mind and due attention is given to both scientific and spiritual knowledge, humanity is liberated from the traps of ignorance and passivity. Indeed, the full range of humanity's powers can be cultivated and released for the progress of the individual and society.

Bahá'u'lláh's instruction to make Bahá'í Temples "as perfect as possible in the world of being" has inspired advances in architecture, design, and engineering. The Bahá'í House of Worship for South America, completed near Santiago, Chile, in October 2016, required the development of a new approach to casting glass to create nine wing-like sheaths with the strength of stone and the luminescent quality of glass.

The eternal journey of the soul

"The soul is a sign of God, a heavenly gem whose reality the most learned of men hath failed to grasp, and whose mystery no mind, however acute, can ever hope to unravel."

— BAHÁ'U'LLÁH

Bahá'u'lláh affirmed that each human being possesses a distinct, rational soul that constitutes the real self. The soul has its origin in the spiritual worlds of God. It is created in the image and likeness of God, meaning that it is capable of acquiring divine qualities and heavenly attributes. The individual soul begins its association with the human being at the time of conception, but the association is not material; the soul does not enter or leave the body and does not occupy physical space.

The soul shows itself through the powers of the mind and the qualities of character that we associate with each person. The expressions of the soul are love and compassion, faith and courage, rational thought and imagination, and other such human qualities that cannot be fully explained by considering a human being as an animal or as a sophisticated organic machine.

Our soul is nourished in prayer. As stated in the Bahá'í writings:

> *For the core of religious faith is that mystic feeling that unites man with God. This state of spiritual communion can be brought about and maintained by means of meditation and prayer.... The Bahá'í Faith, like all other Divine religions, is thus fundamentally mystic in character. Its chief goal is the development of the individual and society, through the acquisition of spiritual virtues and powers. It is the soul of man that has first to be fed. And this spiritual nourishment prayer can best provide.*

When death occurs, the body returns to the world of dust, while the soul continues to progress towards God. Bahá'u'lláh wrote that the soul "will manifest the signs of God and His attributes, and will reveal His loving kindness and bounty."

The exact nature of the afterlife remains a mystery. "The nature of the soul after death can never be described," wrote Bahá'u'lláh. Heaven may be understood as a state of relative nearness to God; hell as a state of remoteness from God. One's degree of nearness to God follows as a natural consequence of his or her efforts to develop spiritually, and also depends on the grace and bounty of God.

Entry into the next life has the potential to bring great joy. Bahá'u'lláh likened death to the process of birth. He explained: "The world beyond is as different from this world as this world is different from that of the child while still in the womb of its mother." Just as the womb constitutes the place for a person's initial physical development, the physical world provides the matrix for the development of the individual soul. During this earthly physical existence, one can develop the spiritual qualities that will be needed in the next life, which is a spiritual existence.

A new calendar: marking time with the attributes of God

Since the earliest beginnings of human history, the measurement of time has been fundamental to the organization of societies. The adoption of a new calendar in each religious era is a symbol of the power of divine revelation to reshape human perception of material, social, and spiritual reality. Through it, sacred moments are distinguished, humanity's place in time and space reimagined, and the rhythm of life recast.

The Bahá'í Faith has its own calendar, the Badí' Calendar, the final provisions of which were adopted globally in 2015. The Badí' Calendar is a solar calendar of 19 months of 19 days each. Either four or five intercalary days round out the solar year. These festive days, known as Ayyám-i-Há, are for celebrating, gift-giving, and performing acts of charity. They occur before a month of daytime fasting which is considered as spiritual preparation for the New Year. The Bahá'í New Year, called Naw-Rúz, falls on the first day of spring in the Northern Hemisphere, the vernal equinox.

Each of the days, months, years, and cycles of the Badí' Calendar is named after a divine attribute, such as Beauty, Mercy, or Splendor. Nine days associated with historical events of the Faith are designated as Holy Days.

MONTHS

1 SPLENDOR
Bahá

2 GLORY
Jalál

3 BEAUTY
Jamál

4 GRANDEUR
'Azamat

5 LIGHT
Núr

6 MERCY
Rahmat

7 WORDS
Kalimát

8 PERFECTION
Kamál

9 NAMES
Asmá'

10 MIGHT
'Izzat

11 WILL
Mashíyyat

12 KNOWLEDGE
'Ilm

13 POWER
Qudrat

14 SPEECH
Qawl

15 QUESTIONS
Masá'il

16 HONOR
Sharaf

17 SOVEREIGNTY
Sultán

18 DOMINION
Mulk

INTERCALARY DAYS
Ayyám-i-Há

19 LOFTINESS
'Alá'

SELECTION OF BAHÁ'U'LLÁH'S

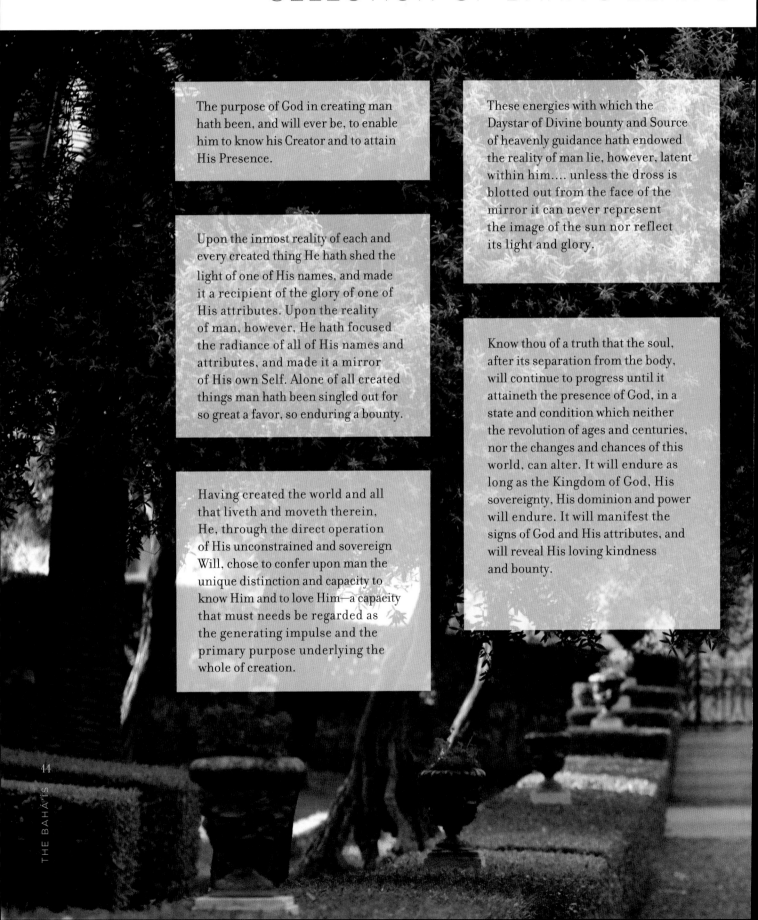

The purpose of God in creating man hath been, and will ever be, to enable him to know his Creator and to attain His Presence.

Upon the inmost reality of each and every created thing He hath shed the light of one of His names, and made it a recipient of the glory of one of His attributes. Upon the reality of man, however, He hath focused the radiance of all of His names and attributes, and made it a mirror of His own Self. Alone of all created things man hath been singled out for so great a favor, so enduring a bounty.

Having created the world and all that liveth and moveth therein, He, through the direct operation of His unconstrained and sovereign Will, chose to confer upon man the unique distinction and capacity to know Him and to love Him—a capacity that must needs be regarded as the generating impulse and the primary purpose underlying the whole of creation.

These energies with which the Daystar of Divine bounty and Source of heavenly guidance hath endowed the reality of man lie, however, latent within him…. unless the dross is blotted out from the face of the mirror it can never represent the image of the sun nor reflect its light and glory.

Know thou of a truth that the soul, after its separation from the body, will continue to progress until it attaineth the presence of God, in a state and condition which neither the revolution of ages and centuries, nor the changes and chances of this world, can alter. It will endure as long as the Kingdom of God, His sovereignty, His dominion and power will endure. It will manifest the signs of God and His attributes, and will reveal His loving kindness and bounty.

WRITINGS ON HUMAN NATURE

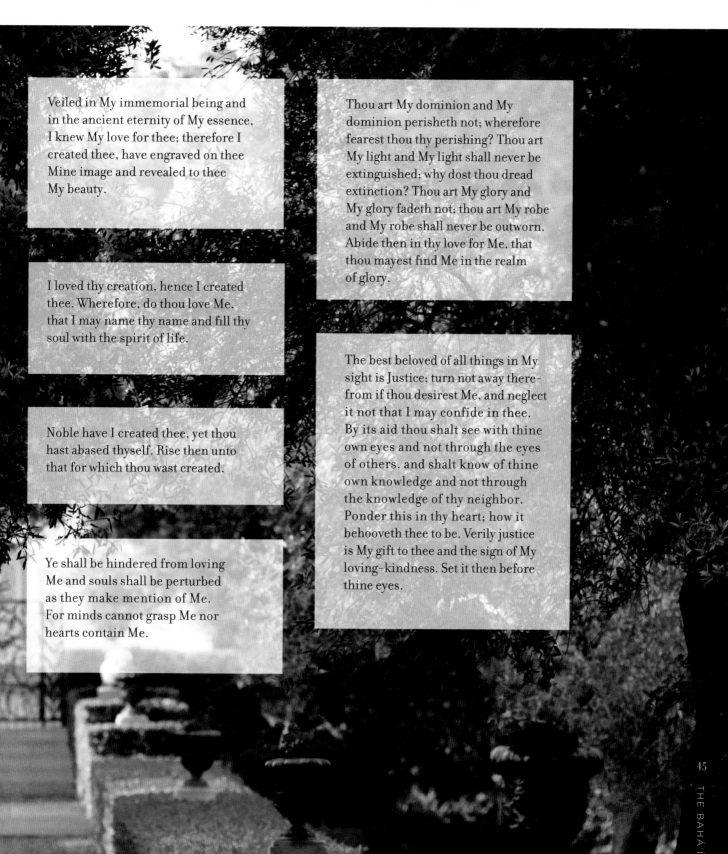

Veiled in My immemorial being and in the ancient eternity of My essence, I knew My love for thee; therefore I created thee, have engraved on thee Mine image and revealed to thee My beauty.

I loved thy creation, hence I created thee. Wherefore, do thou love Me, that I may name thy name and fill thy soul with the spirit of life.

Noble have I created thee, yet thou hast abased thyself. Rise then unto that for which thou wast created.

Ye shall be hindered from loving Me and souls shall be perturbed as they make mention of Me. For minds cannot grasp Me nor hearts contain Me.

Thou art My dominion and My dominion perisheth not; wherefore fearest thou thy perishing? Thou art My light and My light shall never be extinguished; why dost thou dread extinction? Thou art My glory and My glory fadeth not; thou art My robe and My robe shall never be outworn. Abide then in thy love for Me, that thou mayest find Me in the realm of glory.

The best beloved of all things in My sight is Justice; turn not away there-from if thou desirest Me, and neglect it not that I may confide in thee. By its aid thou shalt see with thine own eyes and not through the eyes of others, and shalt know of thine own knowledge and not through the knowledge of thy neighbor. Ponder this in thy heart; how it behooveth thee to be. Verily justice is My gift to thee and the sign of My loving-kindness. Set it then before thine eyes.

BELIEF
in
Action

I n the Bahá'í teachings, refining one's inner character and offering service to humanity are inseparable. This twofold moral purpose helps to shape the endeavors of Bahá'ís in all areas of life.

"We must strive unceasingly and without rest to accomplish the development of the spiritual nature in man, and endeavor with tireless energy to advance humanity toward the nobility of its true and intended station."

—'ABDU'L-BAHÁ

Character and conduct

Central to our spiritual journey is the development of qualities that assist each of us in our progress towards God. In this world, the cultivation of such qualities requires an ongoing refinement of our conduct so that our actions increasingly reflect the nobility and integrity with which every human being is endowed. As we allow the knowledge of God to increase in our minds and hearts, the qualities of our higher nature begin to flourish. With greater and greater clarity, we discern that which leads to nobility and that which leads to abasement.

Each Manifestation of God, as a Divine Educator, brings a new set of laws governing the spiritual and social aspects of life for humanity's particular stage of evolution. Bahá'u'lláh revealed laws governing personal behavior in such areas as prayer, fasting, marriage, and the avoidance of alcohol and drugs. He condemned backbiting, set out the importance of engaging in a trade or profession, and emphasized the importance of educating children. He underscored the virtues of truthfulness, trustworthiness, hospitality, courtesy, forbearance, justice, and fairness.

Bahá'ís understand that divine law cannot be reduced to a simple list of do's and don'ts. Rather, they strive to focus on the transformative power of Bahá'u'lláh's teachings to bring joy, refine character, and revitalize society.

Walking a spiritual path

The Bahá'í teachings emphasize that each person is in charge of his or her own spiritual development. There is no clergy in the Bahá'í Faith. The Bahá'í community can neither be described in terms of a pastor and congregation, nor as a body of believers led by learned individuals endowed with authority to interpret scriptures. While Bahá'í institutions offer guidance and support, and the Bahá'í community is a source of love and encouragement, the responsibility for engaging with the Word of God and for spiritual growth ultimately rests with each individual.

Bahá'ís have come to describe the individual journey as walking a path of service towards God. It is a path open to all of humanity — a path, Bahá'ís believe, that will allow us to build a better world together. Certain aspects are clear: that simply focusing on oneself proves counterproductive; that the path is to be walked in the company of others — each giving and receiving love, assistance, and encouragement; that the tendency to allow self-righteousness to take hold needs to be conscientiously resisted; and that humility is a requisite of progress. No one walking this spiritual path can claim perfection.

Consultation: A collective approach to decision making

In order to build unity and make decisions, Bahá'ís employ the principles and methods of "consultation," a non-adversarial process understood as a collective search for truth. The consultative spirit is one of loving encouragement and respect for all voices, where participation is both frank and courteous. It is animated by a selflessness that discards the notion of ownership of ideas. Once an idea is offered, it belongs to the group.

Members of elected Bahá'í institutions, couples, families, and other groups consult in order to reach a decision or to come to a deeper understanding of a question. Any group seeking to build consensus while strengthening unity may discover new insights through consultation. Consultation does not raise mere opinion to the status of fact or define truth as the compromise between opposing interest groups.

In an elected Bahá'í body, if a unanimous conclusion cannot be reached, a vote may be taken. All members then wholeheartedly support implementation of the decision, regardless of their original view. Without a lingering "opposition," the wisdom of the decision will readily become apparent and the matter may be reconsidered as necessary.

The ideals of consultation call for continually developing one's personal qualities conducive to listening, reflection, and expression. Bahá'u'lláh wrote, "The heaven of divine wisdom is illumined with the two luminaries of consultation and compassion. Take ye counsel together in all matters, inasmuch as consultation is the lamp of guidance which leadeth the way, and is the bestower of understanding."

"Let each morn be better than its eve and each morrow richer than its yesterday."

—BAHÁ'U'LLÁH

Community building infused with spirit

Around the world, people of all ages, faiths, and backgrounds are engaged in a process of community building based on the unifying teachings of Bahá'u'lláh.

Through a process of prayerful study, consultation, action, and reflection, children, youth, and adults engage in their own spiritual development. They explore spiritual concepts together and apply them in their own communities. Capacities for service are developed and increasingly complex collective action becomes possible. Transformation of self and society go hand in hand.

Devotions in the Bahá'í House of Worship in New Delhi, India

Devotional life

The spirit of fellowship and harmony that binds us together is strengthened through acts of worship. Bahá'ís consider daily prayer as essential for spiritual sustenance and growth, just as food is essential for physical sustenance. Through prayer, one praises God, expresses love for Him, or beseeches Him for insight or assistance.

The writings of the Báb, Bahá'u'lláh, and 'Abdu'l-Bahá include many beautiful, expressive, and spiritually powerful prayers which are recited both in private and at devotional gatherings.

It is a common practice for Bahá'ís to gather with their friends and neighbors to offer prayers. Devotional gatherings are held in community centers or in one another's homes and consist largely of reading prayers and passages from holy scriptures in an informal, yet respectful, atmosphere. Uplifting music and song are often included. There are no rituals; no individual has a special role. These simple gatherings bring people of all backgrounds and beliefs together in prayer and generate a unifying spirit that begins to permeate the community.

"Gather ye together with the utmost joy and fellowship and recite the verses revealed by the merciful Lord. By so doing the doors to true knowledge will be opened to your inner beings, and ye will then feel your souls endowed with steadfastness and your hearts filled with radiant joy."

—BAHÁ'U'LLÁH

"As a person cultivates the habit of study and deep reflection upon the Creative Word, this process of transformation reveals itself in an ability to express one's understanding of profound concepts and to explore spiritual reality in conversations of significance."

—THE UNIVERSAL HOUSE OF JUSTICE

The training institute

The words of the Manifestations of God, as found in the world's sacred scriptures, have a creative and transformative effect on the human soul. Interaction with the Word of God—both individually and collectively—releases powerful spiritual and moral forces that inevitably find expression in new social relations, revitalized institutions, and a vibrant community life. A process of personal and social transformation begins with deep reflection on the Creative Word linked with acts of service to humanity. To systematically foster these processes and enable the participation of ever-larger numbers of people, the concept of the "training institute" was adopted worldwide in the mid-1990s.

The nature of the training institute can be understood by imagining an ongoing conversation taking place among friends in thousands upon thousands of social spaces—neighborhoods, villages, schools, universities, and workplaces. The training institute functions as a system of distance education to fuel and facilitate this evolving conversation. The principal elements of the system include the study circle, the tutor, and a set of materials grounded in the Bahá'í writings that express the spiritual insights and knowledge gained in the process of translating Bahá'u'lláh's teachings into reality.

Study circles

A study circle is a small group that meets perhaps once a week for a few hours, usually in the home of one of its members, to study the course materials. The materials include passages from the Bahá'í writings related to specific themes and acts of service. Among the questions participants explore are how to create environments that put people in contact with the spiritual forces released through prayer and devotion; how to strengthen bonds of friendship and establish meaningful patterns of communication among people of various backgrounds; how to make the education of children an integral part of community life; how to help young people develop their intellectual and spiritual capacities; and how to generate dynamics within the family unit that give rise to material and spiritual prosperity.

In response to the materials they study and with support from their institutions, participants arise to carry out specific acts of service. Men and women, young and old alike, come to recognize that they have the power to re-create the world around them. As more and more people become committed to the vision of individual and collective transformation fostered by the institute courses, capacity is gradually built in the community to reflect a pattern of life that places at its heart service and worship.

A selection of courses from the training institute that focus on building capacity to walk a path of service

Reflections on the Life of the Spirit

The Creative Word, the nature of prayer, and the mystery of life after death

Arising to Serve

The path of service and the essential features of community life

Teaching Children's Classes

The transformative effect of the spiritual education of children

Releasing the Powers of Junior Youth

The spiritual empowerment
of adolescents ages 12 to 15

Walking Together on a Path of Service

The training of tutors who assist others
to advance through the sequence
of courses

Building Vibrant Communities

Accompanying one another
on a path of service and consultation

"The light of a good character surpasseth the light of the sun."

—BAHÁ'U'LLÁH

The period of youth

Youth have played a vital role in Bahá'í history from its very start. The Báb declared His mission when He was only 25 years old, and many of His followers were in the prime of their youth when they embraced His teachings.

Likewise, young people were at the forefront of efforts to proclaim the message of Bahá'u'lláh and to share His teachings with others. The Bahá'í teachings encourage young people to see this dynamic period of their lives as a time to make decisive contributions to their communities.

Young people have energy, idealism, and the desire to contribute to the betterment of the world, regardless of their social situations. They can learn to look at the environments in which they interact with others—the family, the peer group, the school, the workplace, the media, the community—and recognize the social forces that operate in them. Forces such as love for truth, thirst for knowledge, and attraction to beauty impel them towards service to humanity. Other forces, such as

spreading materialism and self-centered-ness, are destructive and distort young people's views of the world, thereby impeding individual and collective growth.

Naturally, many matters occupy young people's time and energy: education, work, leisure, spiritual life, physical health. Failure to approach one's life as a coherent whole can breed anxiety and confusion. Through selfless service, however, young people can learn to foster a life in which these various aspects complement each other. By developing patterns of behavior that balance the spiritual and material require-ments of life, they discover both personal growth and meaning.

By developing spiritual perception, the power of expression, and a moral framework, youth are empowered to live a life free of contradictions and contribute to an ever-advancing civilization.

Junior youth spiritual empowerment program

The Junior Youth Spiritual Empowerment Program is a global movement that motivates young people aged 12 to 15 to work together with parents and community members to contribute to the well-being of their neighborhoods and the world at large.

The program is founded on the idea that, to help young people achieve their highest potential, education needs to address both their intellectual and spiritual development. While inspired by the Bahá'í Faith, the program does not approach education in the mode of religious instruction. It affirms that young people have a vital role to play in helping communities grow.

In these groups, junior youth are mentored by older teens and young adults, referred to as "animators," to develop their spiritual qualities, intellectual capabilities, and capacity to serve society. Each week, animators and junior youth study materials based on moral and spiritual concepts and talk about how to navigate a complex world, resist negative forces in their lives, and promote social progress. They engage in meaningful discussions and artistic expression (through drama, cooperative games, visual arts, and storytelling) and acts of community service, all of which help them form strong moral identities.

Animators strive to awaken junior youth to their own potential, channel their energies, and develop their talents to serve their neighbors, family, and friends. Along the way, many animators discover that the Junior Youth Spiritual Empowerment Program makes an impact in their own lives as well as in the lives of the young people they serve.

Families and children

Bahá'ís view the family as the nucleus of human society and family life as the primary place to develop values and capacities essential to the betterment of society. The moral and spiritual education of children assumes vital importance in a world where the joy and innocence of childhood can so easily be overwhelmed by materialism.

The Bahá'í ideal is a family life that cultivates a loving and respectful relationship between parents and children and promotes the principles of consultation and harmony in decision making.

The teachings emphasize the importance of the education of women and girls, both for their own advancement and because it is through educated mothers that the benefits of knowledge can be most effectively and rapidly diffused throughout society.

Ultimately, the aim is for children to increasingly grow up free from all forms of prejudice, recognizing the oneness of humanity and appreciating the innate dignity and nobility of every human being. Bahá'u'lláh called on us to regard one another as "the fruits of one tree and the leaves of one branch." Inspired by this vision, Bahá'ís partner with their neighbors, friends, and colleagues to create programs for the spiritual education of children.

"Regard man as a mine rich in gems of inestimable value. Education can, alone, cause it to reveal its treasures, and enable mankind to benefit therefrom."

— BAHÁ'U'LLÁH

The light-filled interior dome of the Bahá'í House of Worship for South America. The center inscription is a prayer meaning *"O Thou the Glory of the Most Glorious!"*

A gathering at the Bahá'í House of Worship in Apia, Samoa

Bahá'í Houses of Worship

The Bahá'í Houses of Worship around the world are dedicated to joining the worship of God with service to humanity. There are eight regional or continental Bahá'í Temples, located in Australia, Chile, Germany, India, Panama, Samoa, Uganda, and the United States. These structures are open to all people and collectively receive millions of visitors each year.

Each House of Worship has its own distinctive architecture influenced by the local land-scape and culture. Each also has elements that reflect Bahá'í belief: a circular design and nine entrances welcoming people from all directions, a single dome sheltering all under the embrace of one God, and lovely gardens that reflect unity in diversity.

The Bahá'í Faith has no clergy. No sacra-ments, rituals, or sermons take place in the Temple auditoriums. Instead, there are simple devotional programs that include the reciting, singing, or chanting of the Word of God from the Bahá'í sacred scriptures and from the scriptures of other world religions.

Each of these buildings is the central edifice of an institution known as a Mashriqu'l-Adhkár, or "Dawning Place of the Mention of God." In the fullness of time, each Bahá'í House of Worship will be surrounded by other structures dedicated to serving the needs of the community: hospitals, universities, and other humanitarian and social service agencies.

While at present most Bahá'í worship activities take place in homes and local neighborhood centers, national and local Bahá'í Houses of Worship are now being constructed in response to the vitality of the community-building process underway in various parts of the world.

The first of the national Bahá'í Houses of Worship will be in the Democratic Republic of the Congo and Papua New Guinea. The first of the local Bahá'í Houses of Worship are being constructed in Battambang, Cambodia; Bihar Sharif, India; Matunda Soy, Kenya; Norte del Cauca, Colombia; and Tanna, Vanuatu. Sites have been set aside for future Houses of Worship in more than 130 countries.

Yá Bahá'u'l-Abhá
"O Thou the Glory of the Most Glorious!"

This design is a calligraphic arrangement of the invocation "Yá Bahá'u'l-Abhá," an Arabic phrase that can be translated "O Thou the Glory of the Most Glorious!" Known as "the Greatest Name," it is a reference to Bahá'u'lláh and is often displayed in Bahá'í centers and homes.

The ringstone symbol

This design, usually called the ringstone symbol, is frequently engraved on jewelry and may appear on Bahá'í buildings. While the symbol in its entirety is a calligraphic arrangement of the word "Bahá," its vertical line can be interpreted to represent the Holy Spirit proceeding from God through His Manifestations to humanity. The twin stars represent the Báb and Bahá'u'lláh.

Nine-pointed star

A simple nine-pointed star is generally used as a symbol of the Bahá'í Faith. The number nine represents unity, perfection, and completion.

Australia

Sydney, Australia | Dedicated 1961

Overlooking the Pacific coastline and the city of Sydney, the "Angel of Sydney" is surrounded by acres of forests of the Ku-ring-gai Chase National Park.

South America

Santiago, Chile | Dedicated 2016

Nine translucent wings of cast glass and marble rise directly from the ground, giving the impression of floating over large reflecting pools. The Temple is nestled in the foothills of the Andes mountains above the city of Santiago.

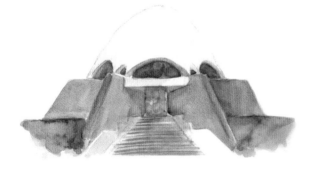

Central America

Panama City, Panama | Dedicated 1972

Its walls ornamented with patterns reminiscent of Mayan-Toltec structures in the Yucatan Peninsula, it stands high on a hill, with the Bay of Panama shimmering in the distance.

Oceania

Apia, Samoa | Dedicated 1984

Its architecture influenced by the life of the Samoan people and surrounding tropical foliage, its simplicity and beauty harmonize with its setting high on a mountain outside the capital city.

Europe

Langenhain, Germany | Dedicated 1964

Crowning a hill in the Taunus region near the city of Frankfurt am Main, its sleek lines are reminiscent of the Bauhaus school of architecture.

Indian Subcontinent

Bahapur, New Delhi, India | Dedicated 1986

The distinctive architecture of the "Lotus of Bahapur" is a symbolic representation of the lotus flower, a motif often appearing in Hindu, Buddhist, and Islamic art and architecture.

North America

Wilmette, Illinois | Dedicated 1953

This Temple is considered the holiest because 'Abdu'l-Bahá, the son of the Founder of the Faith, was directly involved in its planning and laid its cornerstone during His historic sojourn in North America in 1912.

Africa

Kampala, Uganda | Dedicated 1961

Standing on Kikaya Hill on the edge of Lake Victoria, the Temple features flaring eaves and strong use of color—green-tiled dome, exterior in various shades of sandstone brown, and windows of colored glass.

A life of generous giving

The purpose of our lives is to recognize, love, and grow closer to God. We strive to do so, in part, by mirroring God's attributes, such as love, compassion, generosity, justice, and mercy. We fulfill our highest purpose by living a life of service in which we are generous with our love and compassion, and, practically speaking, give freely of our time, energy, knowledge, and financial resources. The impulse to give springs naturally from our gratitude to and love for God. As this gratitude and love fills our hearts, generosity comes to characterize the pattern of our conduct. When we serve others for the love of God, we are motivated neither by the hope of recognition and reward nor by fear of punishment. A life of service to humanity implies humility and detachment, rather than self-interest and ostentation.

Serving humanity

Bahá'ís strive to participate fully in the life of society, working shoulder to shoulder with diverse groups in a wide variety of settings to contribute to the social, material, and spiritual advancement of civilization. Whatever particular form their efforts take, Bahá'ís participate motivated by concern for the common good and with a spirit of humble service to humanity.

Sharing Bahá'í beliefs

When a Bahá'í shares his or her beliefs with another, the act is not an attempt to convince or otherwise prove a particular point. Proselytization is forbidden. Rather, discussing beliefs is an expression of a sincere desire to engage in meaningful conversation about the basic questions of life. "If ye be aware of a certain truth," Bahá'u'lláh has stated, "if ye possess a jewel, of which others are deprived, share it with them in a language of utmost kindliness and goodwill." And further, "A kindly tongue is the lodestone of the hearts of men. It is the bread of the spirit, it clotheth the words with meaning, it is the fountain of the light of wisdom and understanding."

Giving to the Bahá'í funds

Bahá'u'lláh's vision is that humanity will reorganize its affairs to ensure that the vast resources of the planet can be used to bring about spiritual and material prosperity for the entire human race. Within the affairs of their communities, Bahá'ís are learning about how voluntary giving and the moral stewardship of resources can contribute

to development. When Bahá'ís contribute to the funds of the Faith, they see it as a practical way of contributing to constructive processes in the world.

Within the Bahá'í community, funds are established at the local, national, continental, and international levels to which only registered members of the Faith may contribute. This allows the Bahá'í community both to sustain its activity and to channel financial resources in ways that promote the common good. The administration of these funds is entrusted to Bahá'í institutions responsible for making decisions about the allocation of resources on behalf of the community.

Individual Bahá'ís strive to give selflessly and joyfully to the various funds of the Faith, each according to his or her circumstances and means. Contributions are private and voluntary, and soliciting money from individuals is not permitted. Voluntary giving fosters an awareness that managing one's financial affairs in accordance with spiritual principles is an indispensable dimension of a coherently lived life.

"We must be like the fountain or spring that is continually emptying itself of all that it has and is continually being refilled from an invisible source."

—SHOGHI EFFENDI

The Bahá'í Chair for World Peace is an endowed academic program established at the University of Maryland in 1993.

Contributing to the life of society

Bahá'ís are collaborating with an ever-increasing number of movements, organizations, and individuals who further the cause of unity, promote human welfare, and contribute to world solidarity. In choosing areas of collaboration, Bahá'ís bear in mind the principle, enshrined in their teachings, that means should be consistent with ends; noble goals cannot be achieved through unworthy means.

Specifically, it is not possible to build enduring unity through endeavors that require contention or the assumption that inherent conflicts of interest underlie

Community agriculture
project in Mongolia

*"Be anxiously concerned with
the needs of the age ye live in, and
center your deliberations on its
exigencies and requirements."*

— BAHÁ'U'LLÁH

human interactions. Thus, Bahá'ís are not
permitted to take part in partisan politics,
civil disobedience, or violent or
seditious activity.

There are no shortages of opportunities for
collaboration; so many people in the world
today are working intensely towards one or
another aim which Bahá'ís share. Bahá'ís
have been particularly active in advocacy
and education in the areas of human rights,
the advancement of women, and
sustainable development.

Community school in the
Democratic Republic of the Congo

The majority of Bahá'í initiatives for social and economic development are modest in scale and scope and are sustained by resources in the local communities that are carrying them out.

Social action

Bahá'ís engage in social action to promote the social and material well-being of people of all walks of life, whatever their beliefs or background. Such efforts are motivated by the desire to serve humanity and contribute to constructive social change. Social action is pursued with the conviction that every population should be able to mark out the path of its own progress. Social change is not a project that one group of people carries out for the benefit of another.

Fundamentally, Bahá'ís view knowledge as central to social existence, and the perpetuation of ignorance as a severe form of oppression. Every human being has the right of access to knowledge, and the responsibility to participate in its generation, application, and diffusion, according to his or her talents and abilities. The primary concern of social action is to build capacity in individuals and communities to participate in creating a better world.

Bahá'í endeavors for social and economic development fall along a spectrum. The majority of such initiatives are modest in scale and scope and are sustained by resources in the local communities that are carrying them out. Development efforts are usually carried out by small groups of individuals and emerge out of a growing collective consciousness. They are often related to education, health, sanitation, agriculture, or environmental protection. In a few cases, those engaged in grassroots social action are able to extend the range of their activities in an organic fashion, and their efforts evolve into projects of a more sustained nature, with an administrative structure.

Some examples of social action projects around the world, including youth activities, community banks, education, and media.

Zambia

Canada

Bolivia

Brazil

Mongolia

Papua New Guinea

Contributing to public discourse

One aspect of the Bahá'í community's efforts to contribute to the betterment of the world is through participation in the discourses of society.

At any given moment, in social spaces at all levels of society, there are ongoing conversations concerned with various aspects of humanity's well-being and progress: discourses on such subjects as the equality of women and men, peace, governance, public health, and development, to name but a few. Bahá'ís strive to learn with and from others and offer their personal insights, informed by the Bahá'í teachings, to the unfolding discussions.

Individual Bahá'ís—whether through their involvement in the local community, their efforts of social action, or in the course of their studies, occupations, or professional activities—strive to participate fruitfully in such discourses. Bahá'í-inspired agencies contribute to discourses relevant to their work. Bahá'í institutions at the local, national, and international levels engage with governmental and non-governmental bodies to promote ideas conducive to public welfare.

For more than a century, Bahá'ís have contributed to processes of global governance. With the founding of the League of Nations in 1920, Bahá'ís began to establish more formal relations with international organizations. In 1948, the Bahá'í International Community (BIC), representing the Bahá'ís of the world, registered as an international non-governmental organization with the United Nations. The BIC is an active participant in many of the United Nations' major conferences and commissions, frequently presenting papers and statements on such diverse subjects as minority rights, the status of women, crime prevention, and the welfare of children and the family.

At whatever level it occurs, the purpose of Bahá'í participation in discourses is not to persuade others to accept a Bahá'í position on a particular subject. Bahá'ís do not set out to offer any specific solutions to the problems that face humanity, such as climate change, women's health, food production, or poverty alleviation. Nor are efforts pursued as public relations activities or academic exercises. Rather, Bahá'ís strive to learn and engage in genuine conversation. Bahá'ís are eager to share what they are learning in their own efforts to apply Bahá'u'lláh's teachings towards the advancement of civilization and to learn with and from other like-minded individuals and groups.

In September 2000, the Bahá'í representative to the United Nations, acting as the co-chair of the Millennium Forum, addressed world leaders gathered at the U.N. Millennium Summit.

THE BAHÁ'Í INTERNATIONAL COMMUNITY

The Bahá'í International Community (BIC) is a non-governmental organization that represents the worldwide Bahá'í community. It has consultative status with the United Nations Economic and Social Council (ECOSOC) and with the United Nations Children's Fund (UNICEF). Over the past 70 years, the BIC has supported and contributed to UN efforts in the areas of social and sustainable development, gender equality, human rights, and UN reform, among others.

The BIC is also coming to play a more active part in discussions at the regional level and, to this end, has established offices in Addis Ababa, Brussels, and Jakarta.

SCHOLARLY AND PROFESSIONAL CONTRIBUTIONS TO DISCOURSE

One of the ways in which the Bahá'í community is building capacity to contribute meaningfully to public discourse is through seminars for undergraduate and graduate university students. Conducted by the Institute for Studies in Global Prosperity (ISGP) at the national and international levels, these seminars explore subjects especially relevant to students and young professionals.

Around the world, several Associations for Bahá'í Studies provide forums for interested people of all ages and from every field to correlate the Bahá'í teachings with contemporary thought. The Bahá'í Chair for World Peace, established at the University of Maryland in 1993, is an endowed academic program that advances interdisciplinary examination of and discourse on global peace.

69

Creativity and resilience: The Bahá'ís in Iran

A hopeful vision of the transformations underway in the world can seem naive or utopian to some people. Bahá'ís, however, offer more than a vision in words. They offer the testimony of decades of deeds of faith and sacrifice, demonstrating that obstacles can be overcome by bringing to bear spiritual resources of creativity, resilience, and perseverance. This reality is nowhere more evident than in the experience of the Iranian Bahá'í community since the mid-1800s.

From the time of the Báb's announcement of His mission in 1844, the government and clergy of Persia endeavored by every means to stamp out the movement, which has grown to become the largest religious minority in Iran today, with more than 300,000 members. The claims of progressive religious truth and the continuation of divine revelation after Muhammad were seen as heretical. The new Faith's vision of universal education, of decentralized and consultative decision making, of the empowerment of women, and of the mingling of people of all races and religions was seen as deeply disruptive and threatening to the established order. Thus, throughout its history, the Iranian Bahá'í community experienced waves of executions, imprison-

ments, mob violence, confiscation of property, destruction of cemeteries, denial of access to education and many professions, and other forms of systematic repression.

After Iran's 1979 Islamic revolution, the suppression of the Bahá'í community became official government policy, with a documented system of repression chillingly reminiscent of Nazi Germany's Nuremberg Laws that targeted the Jews. In the years following the Islamic revolution, thousands of Bahá'ís, including most of the elected leadership at the local and national levels, were rounded up and imprisoned. Many were tortured and more than 200 were executed.

Yet, Bahá'ís have refused to accept the role of victimhood, or to return violence with violence. The principles of their Faith require obedience to government and forbid violence, sedition, and involvement in partisan political activity. Bahá'ís have instead found creative and resilient ways to put their beliefs into practice. In the early 1900s, Bahá'í schools were established in the capital, as well as in provincial centers— including the Tarbíyat School for Girls, which gained national renown. With the assistance

Left: Street murals are part of an international campaign, "Education is Not a Crime," that calls for education equality in Iran.

Right: American physician, Dr. Susan Moody, with Bahá'í women in Tehran, 1910. Some of these women were among the first to appear in public in Iran without veils.

of American and European Bahá'í helpers, clinics and other medical facilities followed. At the international level, Bahá'ís have worked to strengthen the framework of human rights law and defend the rights of Bahá'ís through education, advocacy, and diplomatic channels.

After the 1979 Islamic revolution, all Bahá'í students and faculty were expelled from Iranian universities. The Bahá'í community appealed to the new Iranian government to ask for justice and redress for the violations of their rights, but the conditions did not change.

In response, the Iranian Bahá'í community started an informal system of college-level education, which has since evolved into the Bahá'í Institute for Higher Education (BIHE). Initially classes were taught in living rooms and kitchens of homes across Iran by Bahá'í academics, many of whom had themselves been barred from teaching professionally. Now taught primarily online, BIHE represents the only chance that Bahá'í youth in Iran have for higher education.

In May 2011, the Iranian government launched a coordinated attack against BIHE, raiding dozens of homes, confiscating computers and materials, and detaining professors and administrators. Since 2011, 16 BIHE educators have been sentenced to four- or five-year prison terms; seven of them remain in prison. Their only crime: educating the youth in their community.

This spirit of constructive resilience is captured in a letter from the Universal House of Justice to the Bahá'í youth in Iran, dated January 29, 2014:

You surely see how throughout the world the light of true religion is fading. Yet, you are the very examples of what illumination this light can bring. You are living proofs that religion promotes upright character, instils forbearance, compassion, forgiveness, magnanimity, high-mindedness. It prohibits harm to others and invites souls to the plane of sacrifice, that they may give of themselves for the good of others. It imparts a world-embracing vision and cleanses the heart from self-centredness and prejudice. It inspires souls to build unity, to endeavour for material and spiritual betterment for all, to see their own happiness in that of others, to advance learning and science, to be an instrument of true joy, and to revive the body of humankind. It burnishes the mirror of the soul until it reflects the qualities of the spirit with which it has been endowed. And then the power of the divine attributes is manifested in the individual and collective lives of humanity and aids the emergence of a new social order. Such is the true conception of religion set forth in the Teachings of Bahá'u'lláh.

"You are living proofs that religion promotes upright character, instils forbearance, compassion, forgiveness, magnanimity, high-mindedness."

—THE UNIVERSAL HOUSE OF JUSTICE

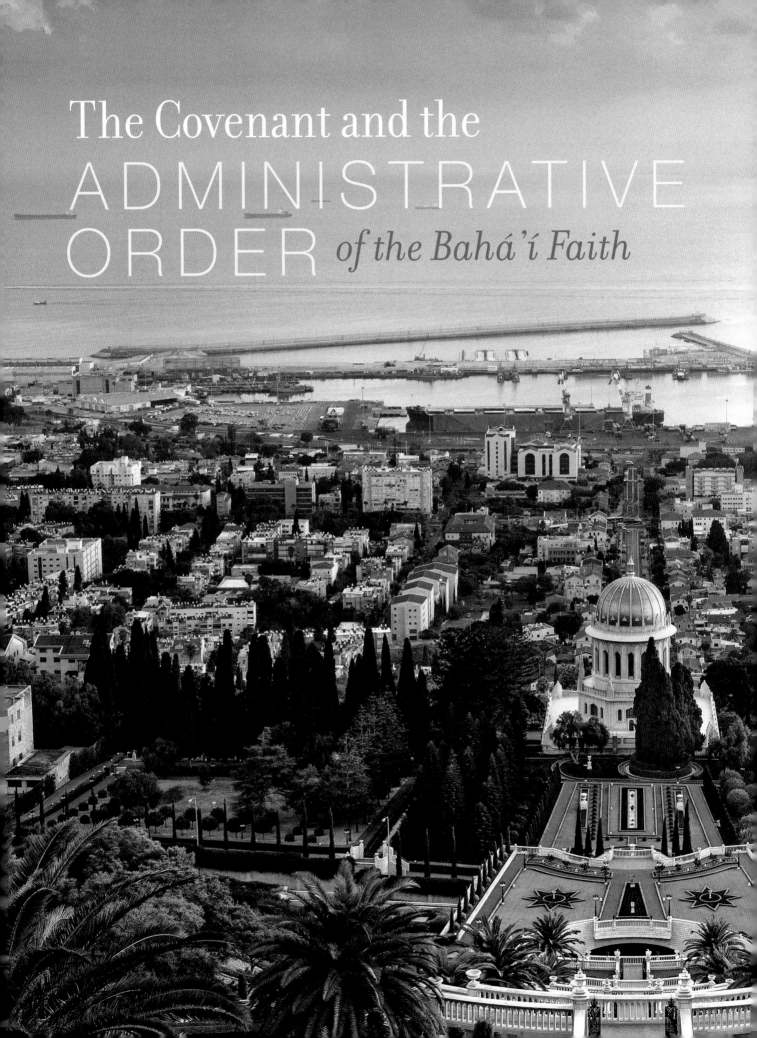

The Covenant and the ADMINISTRATIVE ORDER *of the Bahá'í Faith*

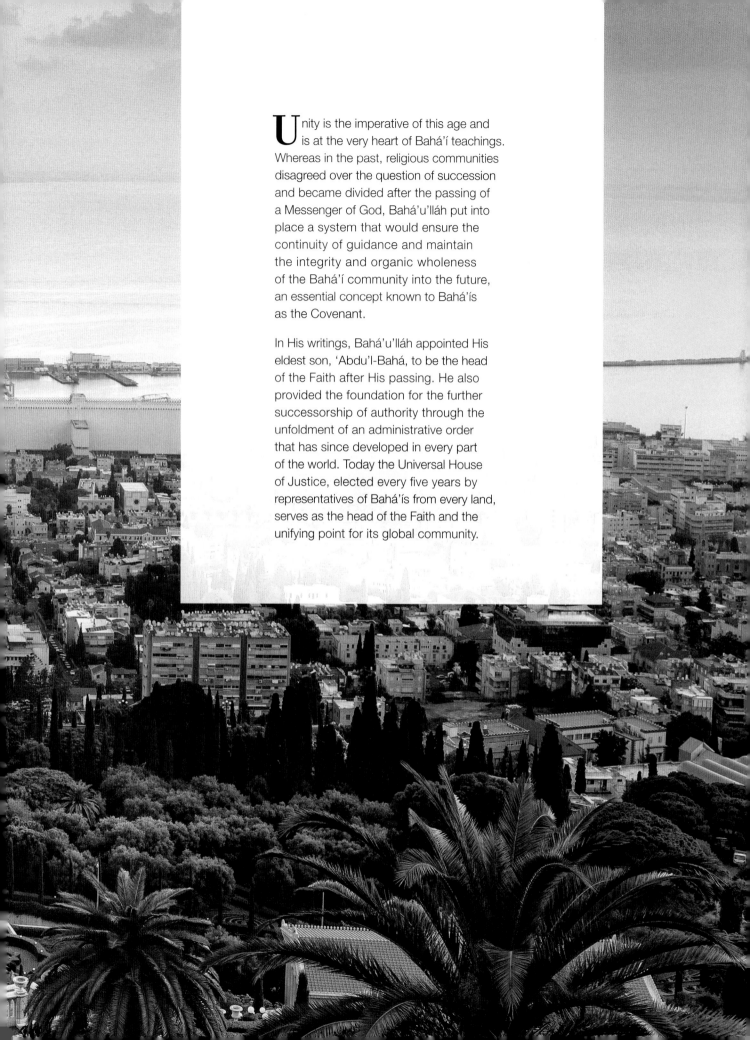

Unity is the imperative of this age and is at the very heart of Bahá'í teachings. Whereas in the past, religious communities disagreed over the question of succession and became divided after the passing of a Messenger of God, Bahá'u'lláh put into place a system that would ensure the continuity of guidance and maintain the integrity and organic wholeness of the Bahá'í community into the future, an essential concept known to Bahá'ís as the Covenant.

In His writings, Bahá'u'lláh appointed His eldest son, 'Abdu'l-Bahá, to be the head of the Faith after His passing. He also provided the foundation for the further successorship of authority through the unfoldment of an administrative order that has since developed in every part of the world. Today the Universal House of Justice, elected every five years by representatives of Bahá'ís from every land, serves as the head of the Faith and the unifying point for its global community.

'Abdu'l-Bahá

Center of the Covenant

"For the first time I saw form noble enough to be a receptacle for the Holy Spirit."

— POET KAHLIL GIBRAN ON MEETING 'ABDU'L-BAHÁ IN NEW YORK IN 1912

'Abdu'l-Bahá was the son of Bahá'u'lláh and the perfect exemplar of the Bahá'í Faith's spirit and teachings. A champion of social justice and an ambassador for international peace, He devoted His life to furthering His Father's cause and to promoting its ideals.

The role 'Abdul-Bahá played as spiritual leader, authoritative interpreter, and role model is unique in all of religious history. Bahá'u'lláh called His son "the Center of My Covenant" and identified 'Abdu'l-Bahá as His successor in His written will, thereby ensuring the unity of the Faith after His passing.

'Abdu'l-Bahá, whose name means "Servant of Bahá," was born in Tehran, Persia, at midnight on May 22, 1844, the very day on which the Báb declared that humanity was entering a new religious cycle.

As a child, He suffered during the government's persecutions of the followers of the Báb. He was only eight years old when Bahá'u'lláh was imprisoned and their home in Tehran was ransacked and confiscated, forcing the entire family to flee. The young 'Abdu'l-Bahá was the first to recognize the potent spiritual change that had occurred in Bahá'u'lláh upon receiving His revelation from God during His imprisonment in Tehran's notorious "Black Pit."

As He grew older, 'Abdu'l-Bahá became His Father's aide and closest companion. 'Abdu'l-Bahá's innate qualities of generosity, intelligence, and humility won Him Bahá'u'lláh's admiration and the title, "The Master."

'Abdu'l-Bahá made His life one of selfless service to others. He often literally gave away the coat off His back. When the early Bahá'ís were banished to the bleak prison-city of 'Akká, many became ill with typhoid fever, malaria, and dysentery. 'Abdu'l-Bahá washed, fed, and comforted them.

Following Bahá'u'lláh's death in 1892, 'Abdu'l-Bahá worked tirelessly to maintain the unity of the followers of the young Bahá'í Faith. He encouraged the establishment of local Bahá'í institutions ordained by Bahá'u'lláh, guided educational, social, and economic initiatives, and brought great prestige to the rapidly expanding Bahá'í community.

Through His travels and many talks and writings, 'Abdu'l-Bahá played a key role in elucidating Bahá'u'lláh's global vision. He had a deep understanding of the spiritual essence of His Father's teachings, and was able to lovingly mirror forth these principles in His own life.

The many stories of His courtesy, kindness, humility, and devotion to God are sources of great inspiration. 'Abdu'l-Bahá's life exemplified how devotion to God finds expression in practical, selfless service.

'Abdu'l-Bahá's travels

In the wake of the Young Turk Revolution of 1908, Ottoman rule of Palestine ended, thereby also ending 'Abdu'l-Bahá's 40-year imprisonment. In 1911, He embarked upon a three-year journey across Europe and North America to share Bahá'u'lláh's teachings. Through His travels, 'Abdu'l-Bahá became the link between the origins of the Bahá'í Faith in the East and the modern embrace of its teachings in the West.

The first public mention of the Bahá'í Faith in North America had been in 1893, at the Parliament of the World's Religions, part of the World's Columbian Exposition in Chicago.

By the time of 'Abdu'l-Bahá's arrival in North America only 19 years later, some 3,000 enthusiastic followers had embraced the Faith.

'Abdu'l-Bahá's travels in the United States and Canada lasted 239 days, during which He visited more than 40 cities. He was greeted with respect and acclaim by Bahá'ís and the general public alike, and was invited to speak to distinguished groups and organizations at universities, in churches and synagogues, and in the homes of prominent individuals.

He called on America to become a land of spiritual distinction and leadership and imparted a powerful vision of America's spiritual destiny in establishing the oneness of humanity. Throughout His visit, 'Abdu'l-Bahá insisted that every venue where He spoke be open to people of all races. To promote the equality of the sexes, on numerous

'Abdu'l-Bahá as a young man

'Abdu'l-Bahá visited Chicago's Lincoln Park during His travels across North America.

Bahá'u'lláh called 'Abdu'l-Bahá

"the Center of My Covenant,"

referring to the leadership role the son was to assume after His Father's death.

occasions He frankly appealed for the rights of women to be recognized. At the Bowery Mission in New York, He personally greeted scores of destitute men with the gift of a coin.

His visit was also distinguished by certain symbolic acts. With His own hands He laid the cornerstone of the Bahá'í House of Worship on the shores of Lake Michigan near Chicago. In a bold demonstration of the Bahá'í principle calling for the elimination of racial prejudice, at a time when such a union was extremely rare and socially unacceptable, He united in marriage two Bahá'ís from different nationalities, one white, the other black. At a dinner with notables in Washington, D.C., He broke

with convention by inviting a Bahá'í African American attorney, Louis G. Gregory, to sit at His right hand.

Before the outbreak of World War I in 1914, 'Abdu'l-Bahá had returned to Palestine. Throughout the war He spent His time acting on the principles that He and His Father had promulgated. He personally organized an extensive agricultural project near Tiberias, which helped to avert a famine.

During the darkest days of the war, in 1916-1917, 'Abdu'l-Bahá revealed the Tablets of the Divine Plan, a series of 14 influential letters addressed to the Bahá'ís of the United States and Canada. These

'Abdu'l-Bahá on May 1, 1912, when He laid the cornerstone for the Bahá'í House of Worship in Wilmette, Illinois.

letters called for the diffusion of the teachings of Bahá'u'lláh and became the charter for the growth of the Bahá'í community throughout the world.

'Abdu'l-Bahá passed away peacefully in His sleep on November 28, 1921, at the age of 77. In His Will and Testament, 'Abdu'l-Bahá appointed His grandson, Shoghi Effendi Rabbani, to succeed Him as the leader, or Guardian, of the Bahá'í Faith. This appointment was an extension of the Covenant established by Bahá'u'lláh.

'Abdu'l-Bahá's travels in North America lasted

239 DAYS
INCLUDING
10 DAYS IN CANADA.

He visited more than

40 CITIES
EAST to WEST.

A vision of the emerging world civilization

The unity of the human race, as envisaged by Bahá'u'lláh, implies the establishment of a world commonwealth in which all nations, races, creeds and classes are closely and permanently united, and in which the autonomy of its state members and the personal freedom and initiative of the individuals that compose them are definitely and completely safeguarded....

A mechanism of world inter-communication will be devised, embracing the whole planet, freed from national hindrances and restrictions, and functioning with marvellous swiftness and perfect regularity.... A world language will either be invented or chosen from among the existing languages and will be taught in the schools of all the federated nations as an auxiliary to their mother tongue.

—"The Unfoldment of World Civilization" 1936

Shoghi Effendi's writings on the world order of Bahá'u'lláh

As Guardian of the Bahá'í Faith, Shoghi Effendi brought an authoritative understanding of the Bahá'í teachings to his writings and translation work. He rendered essential works of Bahá'u'lláh into exquisite English. These authoritative texts have become the basis for translations into numerous other languages.

His writings explain the significance of the Bahá'í administrative order and its contribution to the unified world envisioned by Bahá'u'lláh and help the reader to understand the Faith's growth and development in the context of current world events.

A pattern for future society

For Bahá'u'lláh, we should readily recognize, has not only imbued mankind with a new and regenerating Spirit. He has not merely enunciated certain universal principles, or propounded a particular philosophy, however potent, sound and universal these may be. In addition to these He, as well as 'Abdu'l-Bahá after Him, has, unlike the Dispensations of the past, clearly and specifically laid down a set of Laws, established definite institutions, and provided for the essentials of a Divine Economy. These are destined to be a pattern for future society, a supreme instrument for the establishment of the Most Great Peace, and the one agency for the unification of the world, and the proclamation of the reign of righteousness and justice upon the earth.

—"The World Order of Bahá'u'lláh" 1930

Shoghi Effendi

The Guardian of the Bahá'í Faith

When 'Abdu'l-Bahá passed away in 1921, Shoghi Effendi, His 24-year-old grandson, was a student at Oxford. Shaken by the news, he returned to Palestine to find that 'Abdu'l-Bahá had, in His Will and Testament, appointed him as the Guardian and world head of the Bahá'í Faith. This appointment conferred on him sole authority to interpret and explain the Faith's sacred writings and teachings. He was also charged with furthering the growth of the Bahá'í world community, which he did through a series of progressively more complex plans, each several years in duration. He elaborated on matters such as the organization, election, and functioning of Bahá'í institutions.

Born in 1897 in 'Akká, Shoghi Effendi's thorough education in the Bahá'í teachings was supervised from earliest childhood by his grandfather, with Whom he enjoyed a close relationship. Having acquired a mastery of English, he served for a time as one of 'Abdu'l-Bahá's secretaries.

Through the voluminous guidance they received from Shoghi Effendi, Bahá'ís were able to expand their community to worldwide proportions. By the time of his passing in 1957, nearly 400,000 Bahá'ís resided in more than 200 countries, territories, and colonies. Moreover, the local and national institutional structure of the Faith had been sufficiently developed to enable the first election of the worldwide governing body of the Faith to take place six years later.

Above: Shoghi Effendi in Haifa, 1922

Left: This eagle marks Shoghi Effendi's gravesite in London's New Southgate Cemetery. He passed away in London in 1957 at the age of 60 after a brief and unexpected illness.

The Universal House of Justice

The Universal House of Justice, the international governing body of the Bahá'í Faith, was first elected in 1963.

Bahá'u'lláh ordained this institution in the Kitáb-i-Aqdas, the Most Holy Book, the repository of the laws and ordinances of the Bahá'í Faith. Bahá'u'lláh invested the Universal House of Justice with the authority to legislate on all matters not specifically laid down in the Bahá'í scriptures, and promised that the institution would be inspired by God in its decisions.

The Universal House of Justice is without precedent in religious history. Never before had a Manifestation of God explicitly ordained the establishment of an institution with the mandate to maintain the integrity and flexibility of His religion, safeguard the unity and guide the activities of His followers, and exert a beneficial influence on the life of society.

There is no priesthood within the Bahá'í Faith and none of the members of the Universal House of Justice may claim a special station or authority. Authority is vested in the institution and its collective decision making, not in the individuals elected.

Since 1963, the election of the Universal House of Justice has been held every five years. Every adult Bahá'í is eligible to participate in the election of a delegate to the national convention where their National Spiritual Assembly is elected. Members of all National Assemblies in turn elect the Universal House of Justice. All Bahá'í elections are conducted by secret ballot without nominations, candidacies, or any form of electioneering.

The Universal House of Justice directs the growth and development of the worldwide Bahá'í community through a series of plans that outline goals, approaches, and methods for systematic progress during specific periods of time. Its loving guidance ensures unity of thought and action as the Bahá'í community develops its capacity to participate in the building of a peaceful, just, and prosperous global civilization.

Bahá'í institutions are not merely the means of administering the internal aspects of Bahá'í community life. They are also channels through which the spirit of the Faith flows, uniting and sustaining society as humanity moves towards its collective maturity.

The Seat of the Universal House of Justice on Mount Carmel, in Haifa, Israel.

Appointed and elected institutions

Under the guidance of the Universal House of Justice, elected bodies, known as Local Spiritual Assemblies and National Spiritual Assemblies, tend to the affairs of the Bahá'í community at their respective levels, exercising legislative, executive, and judicial authority. While the Bahá'í Administrative Order places authority in elected bodies, the system also counts on the wisdom and experience of individuals.

An institution of appointed individuals of proven capacity, the Institution of the Counselors, functions under the guidance of the Universal House of Justice, nurturing the Bahá'í community from the grass roots to the international level.

The administrative center of the Bahá'í Faith, on Mount Carmel, Haifa, Israel

HEADS OF THE FAITH AFTER BAHÁ'U'LLÁH'S PASSING

1892–1921	'Abdu'l-Bahá, Center of the Covenant
1921–1957	Shoghi Effendi, Guardian of the Bahá'í Faith
1963	Universal House of Justice first elected

The International Teaching Center at the Bahá'í World Center in Haifa, Israel

The Institution of the Counselors

The Counselors are a highly diverse group of 81 men and women from around the world who inspire and enlighten Bahá'ís in the application of Bahá'u'lláh's teachings in their everyday lives. They encourage action, foster individual initiative, and promote learning. They nurture and advise communities and Spiritual Assemblies so as to empower them to become guiding lights for society at large.

These Counselors are appointed by the Universal House of Justice every five years. They organize their work through five Continental Boards which, in turn, appoint Auxiliary Board members to serve specific geographic areas and territories. The members of the Institution of the Counselors are concerned with enhancing the capacity of the Bahá'í community to devise systematic plans of action, to execute them energetically, and to learn from their experiences. In addition, they nourish bonds of friendship and unity, promote principles and ethical standards enshrined in the Bahá'í teachings, and raise the vision of community members that they may dedicate their energies to the welfare of the human race.

The work of the Continental Boards of Counselors is guided by the nine Counselor members of the International Teaching Center, who are also appointed by the Universal House of Justice for a five-year term. This group pays particular attention to the development of human resources, helping the worldwide Bahá'í community to increase its capacity to endow growing numbers of people with the spiritual insights, knowledge, skills, and abilities required to serve humanity effectively.

Members of National Spiritual Assemblies meet every five years at the Bahá'í World Center in Haifa, Israel, to elect the Universal House of Justice.

National Spiritual Assemblies

The responsibility of fostering the vibrancy of Bahá'í communities at the national level lies with more than 180 National Spiritual Assemblies around the world. These nine-member councils lovingly guide the activities of Bahá'í communities to strengthen their participation in the life of society.

In his writings, Shoghi Effendi, the Guardian of the Bahá'í Faith, likens the functioning of a National Spiritual Assembly to the beating of a healthy heart, "pumping spiritual love, energy and encouragement" to all members of the Bahá'í community. He writes that members of Spiritual Assemblies should "disregard utterly their own likes and dislikes, their personal interests and inclinations, and concentrate their minds upon those measures that will conduce to the welfare and happiness of the Bahá'í Community and promote the common weal." They are to act with "extreme humility" and be known for "their open mindedness, their high sense of justice and duty, their candor, their modesty, their entire devotion to the welfare and interests of the friends, the Cause, and humanity."

National Assemblies channel the community's financial resources, oversee relations with government, and address questions from individuals and Local Spiritual Assemblies. In some countries, they are assisted by elected or appointed Regional Bahá'í Councils, which serve designated geographic areas.

The National Assemblies are elected annually by delegates, who are themselves elected in district or "unit" conventions. Each year, the delegates assemble at national conventions where they consult and share insights about the progress of the Bahá'í community and vote for the nine members of the National Spiritual Assembly. Every five years the members of all National Spiritual Assemblies elect the Universal House of Justice, the international governing body of the Bahá'í Faith.

Members of the first Local Spiritual Assembly
formed in Samoa, 1957

Members of the first Local Spiritual
Assembly of the Bahá'ís of Brussels,
Belgium, 1948

Local Spiritual Assemblies

At the local level, the affairs of the Bahá'í community are administered by the elected nine-member Local Spiritual Assembly. In any town or city where at least nine adult Bahá'ís reside, a Local Assembly may be formed. The Assembly works to promote the spiritual education of children and youth. It safeguards the resources of the community and lovingly encourages the talents and energies of community members.

The Local Spiritual Assembly also organizes the Nineteen Day Feast, the cornerstone of Bahá'í community life, during which Bahá'ís gather for prayer, consultation on the affairs of the community, and fellowship. The Feast is held on the first day of every Bahá'í month. The Bahá'í calendar has 19 months of 19 days each, giving structure and rhythm to community life. The

Universal House of Justice has written that, in addition to its spiritual significance, "the Feast becomes a link that connects the local community in a dynamic relationship with the entire structure of the Administrative Order." The Feast is "an arena of democracy at the very root of society."

The elected Assembly functions as a body and makes decisions through consultation. 'Abdu'l-Bahá writes: "The first condition is absolute love and harmony amongst the members of the assembly. They must be wholly free from estrangement and must manifest in themselves the Unity of God."

Elections are held each April, and Bahá'ís 21 and older are eligible to both vote and be elected. All Bahá'í elections are conducted by secret ballot and are free of nominations, electioneering, and canvassing. Bahá'ís are asked to vote in a spirit of prayer, giving consideration to the moral character and practical ability of the individuals they elect.

85

THE BAHÁ'ÍS

The Bahá'í World Center:
Focal point for a global community

*"Blessed is the spot,
and the house,
and the place,
and the city,
and the heart,
and the mountain,
and the refuge,
and the cave,
and the valley,
and the land,
and the sea,
and the island,
and the meadow
where mention
of God hath been
made, and His
praise glorified."*

— BAHÁ'U'LLÁH

The spiritual and administrative heart of the Bahá'í Faith is situated on the coast of the Mediterranean Sea, in the neighboring cities of 'Akká and Haifa in northern Israel. Both cities are sites of pilgrimage for Bahá'ís, for each is home to the final resting place of one of the Twin Manifestations of God for this day—the Báb and Bahá'u'lláh.

Year round, pilgrims from every corner of the globe come to Their Shrines to pray and meditate. The beauty of these sacred, tranquil places has brought them world renown and together they attract more than a million visitors a year.

'Akká was the final destination of Bahá'u'lláh's successive exiles. On His passing in 1892, His earthly remains were laid to rest in a small building adjacent to the mansion at Bahjí—which is just north of the city and had been His last home. Considered by Bahá'ís as the most sacred spot on earth, the building has gradually been beautified and has become the focal point of a vast, ever-widening circle of magnificently ornamented formal gardens.

Haifa, across the bay from 'Akká, is located on Mount Carmel, venerated since Biblical times. It was here that Bahá'u'lláh indicated that the earthly remains of the martyred Báb should be interred, after 60 years of being transferred from place to place. Today, a Shrine crowns the Báb's final resting place, surrounded by 19 exquisitely landscaped terraces ranging the full height of the mountain.

Further up the mountain and to the side of the Báb's Shrine, arranged along an arc defined by Shoghi Effendi, are the buildings that comprise the Faith's world administrative center. The work of the Bahá'í World Center is conducted by a staff of 700 from more than 75 countries. At the apex of the arc is the Seat of the Universal House of Justice, flanked by the offices of the International Teaching Center, the Center for the Study of the Texts, and the International Bahá'í Archives. The latter two buildings are dedicated, respectively, to the systematic extension of Bahá'í scholarship and the preservation of the Faith's most precious artifacts. ●

The Shrine of the Báb on Mount Carmel with the administrative buildings of the Bahá'í World Center in the background. The Bahá'í shrines, gardens, and buildings in Haifa and neighboring 'Akká have been named UNESCO World Heritage Sites for their "outstanding universal value."

UNIVERSAL
PEACE

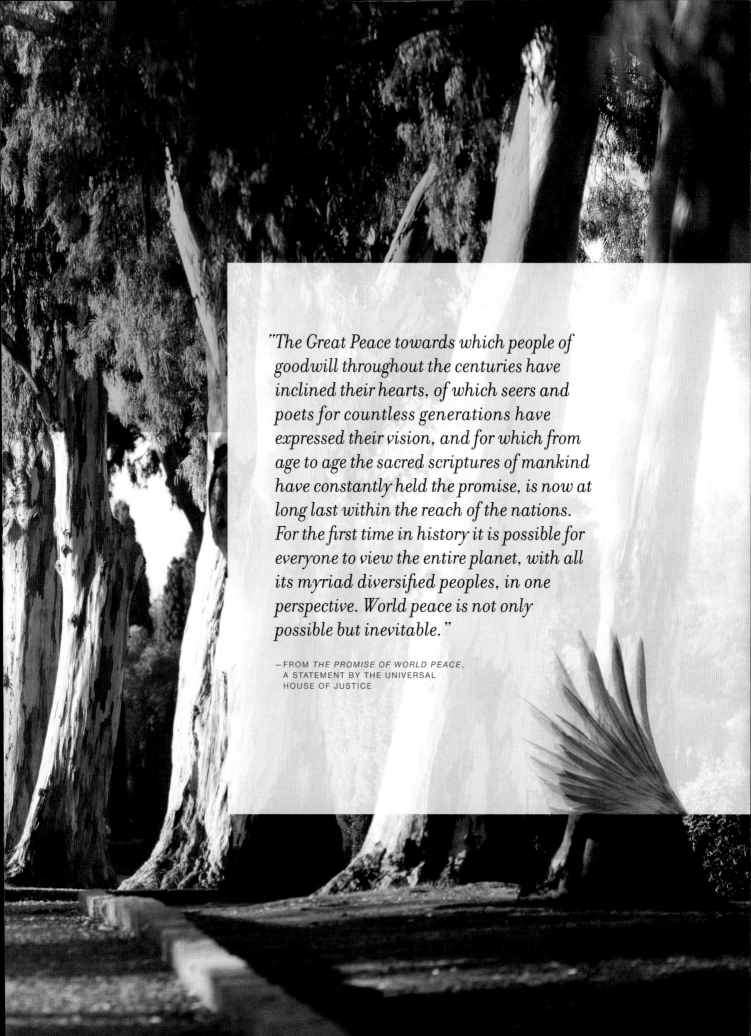

"*The Great Peace towards which people of goodwill throughout the centuries have inclined their hearts, of which seers and poets for countless generations have expressed their vision, and for which from age to age the sacred scriptures of mankind have constantly held the promise, is now at long last within the reach of the nations. For the first time in history it is possible for everyone to view the entire planet, with all its myriad diversified peoples, in one perspective. World peace is not only possible but inevitable.*"

—FROM *THE PROMISE OF WORLD PEACE*,
A STATEMENT BY THE UNIVERSAL
HOUSE OF JUSTICE

The legacy of the twentieth century

Only by understanding the implications of the profound changes that occurred during the last century will humanity be able to meet the challenges that lie ahead. There is no question that the 20th century was one of the most turbulent in human history. The scale of disruption and loss of life due to war and genocide can scarcely be conceived. Stunning advances in science and technology brought great benefits to humanity but also caused severe environmental degradation and raised previously inconceivable ethical challenges. Empires and dynasties were extinguished and long-held beliefs and ideologies discredited. Despite its turbulence, the Bahá'í writings describe this period as "the century of light," referring to the dawning of an awareness of humanity's oneness.

Pangs of death and birth

Shoghi Effendi wrote, "We stand on the threshold of an age whose convulsions proclaim alike the death-pangs of the old order and the birth-pangs of the new." In the chaotic panorama of the 1900s can be seen the operation of two fundamental processes, one of disintegration and the other of integration.

The death-pangs of systems and patterns of thought that divide and degrade humanity are evident. "Hollow and outworn institutions" and "obsolescent doctrines and beliefs" are being "undermined by virtue of their senility, the loss of their cohesive power, and their own inherent corruption." Simultaneously, an integrating process is taking hold, forging contending nations, creeds, classes, and races "through the fire of tribulation" into one organic, harmoniously functioning system. Both processes are accelerating at this critical juncture in history.

"Such simultaneous processes of rise and fall, of integration and disintegration, of order and chaos, with their continuous and reciprocal reactions on each other, are but aspects of a greater Plan," wrote Shoghi Effendi. Humanity has passed through the stages of its infancy and childhood and is now experiencing its turbulent adolescence, standing at the threshold of its collective maturity. Unity of family, of tribe, of city-state and nation has been fully established in preparation for the global system now struggling to be born. Despite the 20th century's horrific toll in war and genocide, its enduring legacy is a humanity coming to grips with itself as one people and the earth as a common homeland.

Candles of unity

'Abdu'l-Bahá used the image of light to capture the transformation of society. Unity, He declared, is the power that illuminates and advances all forms of human endeavor. He referred to the 20th century, then dawning, as "the century of light," observing that in prior times, due to the absence of means, the unity of humanity could not have been achieved.

Now, a century later, we take for granted the communication, transportation, and technology that have merged the continents into one. We readily recognize that self-sufficiency for any nation or people is impossible, that for better or worse all are interdependent. For the first time in human history, the members of the human family can associate with each other, and become familiar with the conditions, beliefs, and thoughts of others far distant. The mechanisms now exist to unite peoples and nations in a single global system.

Beyond the development of material means, 'Abdu'l-Bahá associated "the century of light" with the dawning of a new consciousness—such as the recognition that viewing women as inferior to men is "ignorance and error" and that the advancement of women requires equal rights, education, and opportunity. He identified seven "candles of unity," representing multiple dimensions of progress awakening throughout the East and the West. These foreshadowed developments that grew in strength throughout the 20th century and continue today.

He alluded to sovereign states building unity in the political realm, currently seen in organizations such as the United Nations,

as well as unity of thought in world undertakings, visible in vast programs for development, aid, human rights, or the environment. He highlighted unity in freedom, foreseeing a century which would witness the end of colonialism and the rise of movements for self-determination and democratic rule around the world.

He referred to unity in religion as the "cornerstone of the foundation itself," uniting people in the recognition that God is one and that His religion throughout the ages is one. Unity of nations envisioned today's growing acceptance that, however wide the differences and dire the challenges, all are inhabitants of a single global home-land. Unity of races, "making of all that dwell on earth peoples and kindreds of one race," expresses the foundational principle of the oneness of humanity. And finally, He advanced unity of language, referring to the choice of an auxiliary language enabling all people to converse. These seven "candles of unity" were lit during the 20th century.

Hope and constructive action

Despite the grave threats that still hang over humanity's future, the world has been transformed. A threshold has been crossed from which there is no turning back. The path to peace "will be tortuous," the Universal House of Justice wrote, and people will face "despair and bewilderment" if they do not see the transition in progress. Understanding that we are witnessing the death-pangs of the old order and the birth-pangs of the new, we can bend our energies to the urgent needs of the day, our conviction sustained by the restorative joy, constructive hope, and radiant assurances imparted by Bahá'u'lláh's healing message.

Despite the grave threats that still hang over humanity's future, the world has been transformed by the events of the 20th century. Despite continuing injustices based on gender, race, class, or ethnicity, a threshold has been crossed from which there is no turning back.

UNITY IN THE political realm

UNITY OF thought

UNITY IN freedom

UNITY IN religion

UNITY OF nations

UNITY OF races

UNITY OF language

Requirements for true peace

"World peace is not only possible but inevitable."

—THE UNIVERSAL HOUSE OF JUSTICE

The Bahá'í writings are replete with references to universal peace—"the supreme goal of all mankind"—as well as explanations of the social principles it requires. Among these are the independent search after truth; the oneness of the entire human race; the abolition of all forms of prejudice; the harmony between religion and science; the equality of men and women; the requirement of universal education; the adoption of a universal auxiliary language; the abolition of extremes of wealth and poverty; the institution of a world tribunal for the adjudication of disputes between nations; and the affirmation of justice as the ruling principle in human affairs. Bahá'ís do not view these principles as mere statements of vague aspiration—they are understood as matters of immediate and practical concern for individuals, communities, and institutions alike.

Recognizing the nobility of human nature

One of the most entrenched obstacles to peace is the widespread and uncritical acceptance of the proposition that human beings are incorrigibly selfish and aggressive. The vision of Bahá'u'lláh challenges the assumption that self-interest drives prosperity and that progress depends on its expression through relentless competition. Such views render humans incapable of erecting a social system at once progressive and peaceful, dynamic and harmonious, one that gives free play to individual creativity and initiative and is based on cooperation and reciprocity. Selfishness and aggression, far from expressing humanity's true self, represent a distortion of the human spirit. Deeper awareness of our spiritual nature will inspire new approaches and systems which, because they are consistent with the inherent nobility of humanity, will foster harmony and cooperation instead of competition and conflict.

'Abdu'l-Bahá continues:

Material civilization is like a lamp-glass. Divine civilization is the lamp itself and the glass without the light is dark. Material civilization is like the body. No matter how infinitely graceful, elegant and beautiful it may be, it is dead. Divine civilization is like the spirit, and the body gets its life from the spirit, otherwise it becomes a corpse. It has thus been made evident that the world of mankind is in need of the breaths of the Holy Spirit. Without the spirit the world of mankind is lifeless, and without this light the world of mankind is in utter darkness.

Prosperity, wealth, and poverty

For the material and spiritual dimensions of civilization to advance in harmony, the very notion of prosperity needs to be re-examined. Prosperity cannot be understood as the mere accumulation of personal wealth. Material means are clearly vital to the advancement of civilization, and achieving prosperity implies that all people should have access to such means.

The current extremes of wealth and poverty in the world are becoming ever more untenable. There is an inherent moral dimension to the generation, distribution, and utilization of wealth and resources, which needs to be reflected in more equitable economic structures and voluntary individual behavior. As new patterns emerge, material resources will increasingly be used to facilitate access to knowledge for all people and to uplift and edify the life of the whole of society.

- Independent search after truth

- The oneness of the entire human race

- The abolition of all forms of prejudice

- Harmony between religion and science

- The equality of women and men

- Universal education

- Adoption of a universal auxiliary language

- Abolition of the extremes of wealth and poverty

- The institution of a world tribunal for the adjudication of disputes between nations

- The confirmation of justice as the ruling principle in human affairs

Material and spiritual civilization

True peace is more than the mere cessation of war. The emergence of the materially and spiritually prosperous global civilization associated with humanity's age of maturity requires that the practical and spiritual aspects of life advance harmoniously together. 'Abdu'l-Bahá states that while "material civilization is one of the means for the progress of the world of mankind," until it is "combined with Divine civilization, the desired result, which is the felicity of mankind, will not be attained."

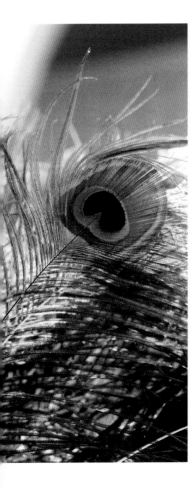

Reorganizing the relationships between individuals, communities, and institutions

As humanity approaches its collective maturity, the need for a new understanding of the relationships between the individual, the community, and the institutions of society becomes ever more pressing. The interdependence of these three protagonists in the advancement of civilization has to be recognized. Old paradigms of conflict in which, for example, institutions demand submission while individuals clamor for freedom, need to be replaced with more profound conceptions of the complementary roles to be played by each in building a better world.

To accept that the individual, the community, and the institutions of society are the protagonists of civilization building, and to act accordingly, opens up great possibilities for human happiness. It allows for the creation of environments in which the exercise of power over others is replaced by the endeavor to release the true powers of the human spirit—powers of love, of justice, and of unified action.

A harmonious relationship with nature

The maturation of the human race requires an organic change in the structure of society, which will fully reflect the interdependence of all its elements, as well as its reciprocal relationship with the natural world that sustains it. Such a change must go hand in hand with a widespread change in the attitudes and behavior of human beings. The inward life of man as well as his outward environment have to be reshaped if human survival is to be secured.

The wealth and wonders of the earth are the common heritage of all people, who deserve just and equitable access to its resources. It is undeniable that the current world order has failed to protect the environment from ruinous damage. Society attaches absolute value to expansion, acquisition, and the constant creation and gratification of wants. Clearly, such goals are not sustainable.

Building new patterns and structures

The vast changes called for in Bahá'u'lláh's teachings must occur in individuals and in the structure of society, at all levels from the family to global institutions. "Is not the object of every Revelation," He proclaimed, "to effect a transformation in the whole character of mankind, a transformation that shall manifest itself, both outwardly and inwardly, that shall affect both its inner life and external conditions?" Bahá'ís and all who share Bahá'u'lláh's vision are working systematically to create the nucleus of a divine civilization—to build new patterns of individual and community life and new organizational structures.

The oneness of humanity is the goal of human progress but must also be understood as its core operating principle. Unity in diversity is not a state that results from first solving all problems; it is rather the means of solving problems, of bringing about deep social transformation. By discovering unifying, inclusive approaches to community building, social action, and public discourse that resonate with the best in human nature, Bahá'í experience is giving rise to new models demonstrating the power and potential inherent in the spirit of the age.

A Summons to Peace

In a statement addressed to the peoples of the world issued in 1985 and titled *The Promise of World Peace*, the Universal House of Justice expressed the sincere and earnest longing of Bahá'ís everywhere to join hands with all people of goodwill in the urgent task of building the foundations of a just, unified, and sustainable world:

In contemplating the supreme importance of the task now challenging the entire world, we bow our heads in humility before the awesome majesty of the divine Creator, Who out of His infinite love has created all humanity from the same stock; exalted the gem-like reality of man; honoured it with intellect and wisdom, nobility and immortality; and conferred upon man the "unique distinction and capacity to know Him and to love Him", a capacity that "must needs be regarded as the generating impulse and the primary purpose underlying the whole of creation."

We hold firmly the conviction that all human beings have been created "to carry forward an ever-advancing civilization"; that "to act like the beasts of the field is unworthy of man"; that the virtues that befit human dignity are trustworthiness, forbearance, mercy, compassion and loving-kindness towards all peoples. We reaffirm the belief that the "potentialities inherent in the station of man, the full measure of his destiny on earth, the innate excellence of his reality, must all be manifested in this promised Day of God." These are the motivations for our unshakeable faith that unity and peace are the attainable goal towards which humanity is striving.

At this writing, the expectant voices of Bahá'ís can be heard despite the persecution they still endure in the land in which their Faith was born. By their example of steadfast hope, they bear witness to the belief that the imminent realization of this age-old dream of peace is now, by virtue of the transforming effects of Bahá'u'lláh's revelation, invested with the force of divine authority. Thus we convey to you not only a vision in words: we summon the power of deeds of faith and sacrifice; we convey the anxious plea of our co-religionists everywhere for peace and unity. We join with all who are the victims of aggression, all who yearn for an end to conflict and contention, all whose devotion to principles of peace and world order promotes the ennobling purposes for which humanity was called into being by an all-loving Creator.

In the earnestness of our desire to impart to you the fervour of our hope and the depth of our confidence, we cite the emphatic promise of Bahá'u'lláh:

"These fruitless strifes, these ruinous wars shall pass away, and the 'Most Great Peace' shall come."

Walking together on a path of service

The worldwide Bahá'í community is warm, vibrant, diverse, and welcoming. We invite you to learn with us how Bahá'u'lláh's teachings are changing the world. We welcome participants of all backgrounds to:

- Join a study circle (The first course is "Reflections on the Life of the Spirit." New groups are always forming.)

- Join a Bahá'í children's class

- Join a group exploring the Junior Youth Spiritual Empowerment Program (for ages 12–15)

- Attend or host an informal devotional gathering

- Learn about Bahá'í service projects in your neighborhood

Start by contacting Bahá'ís in your local community:
www.bahai.org/national-communities/

For further information visit www.bahai.org